Ambition
English Communication III
Workbook

解答・解説

開隆堂

Part 1　基本問題

1 (1) dramatically　(2) categories

(3) internationally　(4) secretly

2 (1) keen　(2) resounded

(3) encourage, to　(4) bout

3 (1) was commonly referred to as

(2) compete against each other

(3) in which Jane used to keep

(4) is keen on playing soccer

4 (1)(例)The anime event attracted a large audience of 25,000 fans.

(2)(例)She felt uncomfortable at the party.

(3)(例)Some people play video games professionally for prize money.

(4)(例)Umehara became a champion at one of the world-famous tournaments.

解説

1 (1) dramatically 副「劇的に」／ dramatic 形「劇的な」 (2) category 名「カテゴリー，部門」。空所前の two から，複数形 categories を選ぶ。 (3) internationally 副「国際的に」／ ironically 副「皮肉にも」 (4) secretly 副「こっそりと」／ commonly 副「一般に」

2 (1) have a keen interest in ～「～に強い関心を持っている」 (2) resound「(音が)響き渡る；(名前などが)知れ渡る」 (3)〈encourage ＋O(人)＋to do〉「人に～するよう励ます[勧める]」 (4) bout「試合，一勝負」

3 (1) refer to A as B「A を B と呼ぶ」の受け身形は A is referred to as B。 (2) compete against ～「～と競う」。compete は自動詞なので，「互いに競い合う」という場合は，前置詞 against が必要。 (3)「これはその中にジェーンが宝石をしまっていた木製の箱です」と考えて，関係代名詞の前に in を置く。

(4) be keen on ～ing「～することに熱心[夢中]である」

4 (1)「(客など)を呼び寄せる」は他動詞の attract で，「～もの大観衆」は a large audience of ～で表す。 (2) feel uncomfortable「居心地が悪い」⇔ feel comfortable「居心地がよい」 (3) professionally 副「プロとして」＜ professional 形「プロの」 (4)「チャンピオンになる」は become a champion。cf. win a championship「チャンピオンの座を獲得する，優勝する」

Part 2　基本問題

1 (1) critical　(2) championship

(3) frequent　(4) skillfully

2 (1) concentration　(2) instantaneous

(3) updated　(4) identified

3 (1) Kaori was invited to dinner

(2) far more difficult than I had expected

(3) spends most of his free time reading

(4) speak not only English but also

4 (1)(例)She dedicated herself to saving poor children.

(2)(例)She realized her real strength was running faster than anybody else.

(3)(例)I became acquainted with many people while (I was) studying abroad.

(4)(例)His novels are very popular both inside and outside his country.

解説

1 (1) critical 形「重大な，批判的な」／ critic 名「批評家」 (2) championship 名「優勝者の地位」／ champion 名「優勝者，チャンピオン」 (3) frequent 動「～に足繁く通う」／ frequently 副「頻繁に」 (4) skillfully 副「うまく，巧みに」／ skillful 形「うまい，巧みな」

2 (1) concentration 名「集中(力)」＜ concentrate 動「集中する」

(2) instantaneous 形「(行動・反応などが)即座の」。類義語の instant は名詞の前にだけ用いるので，ここでは不可。 (3) updated 形「更新された，最新の」 (4) identify with ～「～と自分(の姿)を重ねる，～に共感を覚える」

3(1) be invited to dinner at ～で「～宅の夕食に招待される」という受け身形。 (2)〈far + 形容詞・副詞の比較級〉は「はるかに～」という〈強調〉を表す。than のあとは過去完了形の had expected。 (3)〈spend + O + ～ing〉「O(時間・お金など)を～することに費やす」 (4)〈not only A but also B〉「A だけでなく B もまた」では，内容上の力点は B に置かれる。

4(1) dedicate *oneself* to ～ing「～することに専念[専心]する」 (2) *one's* real strength で「～の本当の力，実力」という意味を表す。「ほかのだれよりも」は than anybody else で表す。 (3) become acquainted with ～「～と知り合いになる」。「海外留学中に」= while (I was) studying abroad では，主節と共通の主語 I と be 動詞の was を省略できる。 (4)「国の内外で」は，「国内と国外の両方で」と考えて，both inside and outside his country で表す。この both は副詞。

Part 3 基本問題

1(1) editing (2) installed
  (3) enrolled (4) withdrawal
2(1) addicted to (2) reversal
  (3) refusal (4) cooperation with
3(1) You are not allowed to take
  (2) enjoying communicating with each other
  (3) have ample opportunity to share
  (4) is designed to teach beginners
4(1)(例)More than 20 percent of Japan's population is over 65 years old.
  (2)(例)She has a wide range of knowledge in astronomy.

(3)(例)You can enjoy various sorts of dishes at the restaurant.
(4)(例)How many hours a day do you practice playing video games?

解説

1(1) editing 名「編集」／ edit 動「編集する」 (2) install 動「～を設置する」／ attach 動「～を添付する」 (3) be enrolled in ～「(学校・講座など)に入学する，登録する」。／ be contained in ～「(容器・場所など)に含まれている，入っている」 (4) withdrawal 名「撤退，途中退場」／ withdraw 動「～から撤退する」

2(1) become addicted to ～「～に対して中毒になる，～の依存症となる」 (2) spend *one's* day-night reversal life「昼夜逆転した生活を送る」 (3) face a refusal「拒否される」。refusal 名「拒否，拒絶」< refuse 動「拒否する，拒絶する」 (4) in cooperation with ～「～と協力して」

3(1) be allowed to *do*「～することを許されている」は〈allow + O + to *do*〉「O が～することを許す」の受け身形。ここでは不定詞の否定形 not to *do* に注意。 (2) enjoy のあとに communicating with each other「互いにコミュニケーションを交わすこと」を続ける。communicate は自動詞なので，前置詞の with が必要。 (3) have opportunity to *do*「～する機会がある」の opportunity の前に ample 形「豊かな，十分な」を置く。 (4) be designed to *do*「～するように考えられて[作られて，設計されて]いる」。〈teach + O(人) + how to *do*〉「人に～のし方を教える」の O の位置に beginners「初心者」を置く。

4(1) more than 20 percent of Japan's population を文の主語にする。〈～ percent of + 名詞〉が主語となる場合，このあとに続く動詞の数は，of のあとの名詞に合わせる。この文では，単数名詞の population に合わせ

て，be 動詞は is を使う。　(2)「〜において幅広い知識を持っている」＝have a wide range of knowledge in 〜。a wide range of のあとには可算名詞・不可算名詞のどちらも置くことができる。　(3)「さまざまな種類の〜」を various sorts of 〜で表す。「料理」は dish を複数形で用いる。　(4)「1 日に何時間〜しますか？」と尋ねる文は，How many hours a day do you 〜？の形。practice は名詞のほか，動名詞（〜ing）も目的語にとる。

Part 4　基本問題

1 (1) honing　(2) logical　(3) strategically
(4) promptly

2 (1) sharpen　(2) purposefully
(3) aspects　(4) initiative

3 (1) in order to win competitive games
(2) for only one and a half hours
(3) Research is needed to find out how
(4) as well as how to grow them

4 (1)（例）The number of public phones is decreasing rapidly in Japan.
(2)（例）Who will be in charge of the art club next year?
(3)（例）He is interested in how children acquire a language.
(4)（例）He expects that his new course will help students improve their writing skills.

解説

1 (1)〈spend＋O＋〜ing〉「O（時間・お金など）を〜することに費やす」の〜ing の位置に来るので，honing が適切。　(2) logical 形「論理的な」／logic 名「論理学，論理」。logical thinking で「論理的思考」という意味。　(3) strategically 副「戦略的に」／strategy 名「戦略」　(4) promptly 副「迅速に」／prompt 形「迅速な」

2 (1) sharpen 動「（刃など）を研ぐ」＜ sharp 形「鋭い」　(2) purposefully 副「目的意識を持って」（≒with a clear aim）　(3) discuss an issue from all aspects「問題についてあらゆる面から議論する」　(4) take the initiative to *do*「率先して〜する」

3 (1)「〜するために」は副詞的用法の〈to＋動詞の原形〉でも表せるが，〈目的〉を明確に述べたい場合は in order to *do* を用いる。　(2)「1 時間半の間だけ」は for only one and a half hours で表す。複数形の hours に注意。　(3)「研究が必要とされる」＝Research is needed を文頭に置き，そのあとに〈目的〉を表す to find out を続ける。疑問詞 how は名詞節（間接疑問）を導く。　(4)〈A as well as B〉「B と同様 A も」では，内容上の力点は A に置かれるのがふつう。

4 (1) the number of 〜「〜の数」は単数扱いなので，このあとに続く be 動詞は is。decrease「減る」⇔increase「増える」　(2) in charge of 〜「〜を担当して」を will be のあとに続ける。　(3) be interested in 〜「〜に興味がある」の in のあとに，名詞ではなく間接疑問を続ける点に注意。「言語を獲得する」は acquire a language で表す。　(4)「…と期待する」は expect that … で表す。that 節の中には〈help＋O（人）＋動詞の原形〉を用いる。

発展問題

(1) ウ
(2) an increase in the number of video gamers
(3) あたかも体の一部であるかのようにスマートフォンをいつでもどこでも持ち歩く（36字）
(4) 家で非常に長い時間を過ごす／ほかのゲーマーたちとリモートで交流し，ストレスから逃れる
(5) イ

解説

(1) 第1段落第2～3文で，約80億人の世界人口に対して，世界のビデオゲーム人口は37億人であると述べている。この数字を「おおざっぱに」とらえれば，「世界人口の半分近くがビデオゲームで遊んでいる」と言えるので，ウのroughlyを選んで, roughly speaking「おおざっぱに[おおまかに]言えば」とする。

(2) 下線部②のitは，第2段落第1文で述べている「ビデオゲーム人口の増加」を指す。

(3) 第3段落第2文後半のmany people carry … part of their body の内容を答える。as if it were part of their body は〈as if＋仮定法過去〉で，「あたかもそれ(＝スマートフォン)が体の一部であるかのように」という意味。

(4) 下線部④のあとの内容と合うように，空所に日本語を補う。be forced to do は「～することを余儀なくされる」。〈provide A with B〉は「A(人)にB(もの)を提供する」という意味の重要熟語。

(5) ア　選択肢の訳「世界のビデオゲーム人口が増加しているにもかかわらず，ビデオゲーム産業の規模はそれほど著しく成長していない」　第1段落第4～5文で「世界のビデオゲーム人口の増加に伴い，ビデオゲーム産業の規模も拡大しつつある」ことを述べているので，選択肢アは誤り。　イ　選択肢の訳「最近では，パソコンはゲーマーの間で選ばれることが最も少ない選択肢であり，スマートフォンやゲーム機に後れを取っている」　第2段落第5～6文の内容と一致。ゲーマーがゲームをするのに使う機器は，第1位がスマートフォンで約70パーセント，第2位がゲームコンソールで52パーセント，第3位がパソコンで43パーセントである。　ウ　選択肢の訳「モバイルゲームの問題の1つは，すべてのゲームが若い人たちの好みに合わせて作られていることである」　第3段

落第4文の people of different age groups can find their favorite games という内容と矛盾。　エ　選択肢の訳「COVID-19 パンデミックの間，ロックダウンのためにモバイルゲーム業界は人気が低下した」　第4段落第1文によれば，すべてのゲーム・プラットフォームの中でモバイル・ゲームが「最も大きな成長を遂げた」(experienced the most significant growth)ことがわかるので，選択肢エは誤り。

＜全訳＞

　ビデオゲームで遊ぶことは，現代社会において人気のあるアクティビティとなっている。世界のビデオゲーム人口は毎年着実に増加しており，2023年現在，全世界には約37億人のビデオゲーマーがいると推定されている。世界人口は約80億人なので，①大まかに言えば世界人口の半分近くがビデオゲームで遊んでいることになる。世界のビデオゲーム人口が増加するに従って，ビデオゲーム産業の規模も拡大しつつある。今やビデオゲーム産業は，スポーツ産業と映画産業を合わせたよりも多くのお金を稼いでいる。

　これほどまでにビデオゲーム人口が増加している原因は何であろうか。モバイル機器の普及が②これに大きく貢献しているのは間違いない。かつてはビデオゲーマーと言えばパソコンやゲーム機を連想する人が多かったかもしれない。しかし最近では，ビデオゲーマーのうち最も急成長を遂げている層はモバイル機器，特にスマートフォンへとシフトしているのだ。最新の調査によれば，約70パーセントの人がスマートフォンでビデオゲームをプレイするのを好んでいる。2位はゲーム機で52パーセント，3位はパソコンで43パーセントである。

　モバイルゲーミングの人気の最大の理由の1つは，③そのアクセスのしやすさにある。スマートフォンが一般的なデバイスとなった現在では，多くの人々があたかも体の一部であるかのように，スマートフォンをいつでもどこでも持ち歩いている。彼らは電車やバスに乗っている間の隙間時間をスマートフォンでビデオゲームをプレイして過ごす。それに加えて，多くのアクションを含むアドベンチャーから頭を使うパズルまで，幅広い種類のモバイル・ゲームが提供されているので，さまざまな年齢層の人々がお気に入りのゲームを見つけることができる。そのおかげで，彼らにとってゲームをすることは楽しい経験となるのである。

COVID-19 パンデミックの間，あらゆるゲーム・プラットフォームが好景気にわいたが，なかでもモバイル・ゲームは最も大きな成長を遂げた。_④ロックダウンにより，人々は家で非常に長い時間を過ごすことを余儀なくされた。皮肉なことに，モバイル・ゲームをプレイすることで，人々はほかのゲーマーたちとリモートで交流し，ストレスから逃れることができたのだ。

Lesson 2 (pp.10-15)

Scott Gende and Thomas Quinn's Report on Salmon and Bears

Part 1　基本問題

1(1) Fisheries　(2) collapse
　(3) findings　(4) derived

2(1) scooped up　(2) array
　(3) wreaked, on　(4) came about
　(5) died down

3(1) makes a lot of contributions to
　(2) The salmon carcasses discarded by bears result in
　(3) unless they are protected carefully

4(1)(例)We visited the beautiful village by the lake, where we stayed for a week.
　(2)(例)Few people know the truth of the incident.
　(3)(例)His career as a journalist has spanned more than three decades.
　(4)(例)the result was that he scored the highest marks in the class

解説

1(1) fishing 名「釣り」／ fisheries(fishery の複数形)名「漁業」　(2) collapse 名「崩壊，(経済的)破綻」／ carcass 名「(動物の)死体，死骸」　(3) finding 名「発見したもの，(研究などで)わかったこと」／ seeing 名「見ること，視覚」　(4) deprive 動「奪う」／ derive 動「引き出す」。be derived from ～で「～に由来する」という意味。

2(1) scoop up「～をくみ上げる，すくい上げる」　(2) an array of ～「ずらりと並んだ～，たくさんの～」　(3) wreak ～ on …「…に(損害・破壊など)をもたらす，引き起こす」　(4) come about「(出来事が)起こる」。cf. bring about ～「～を引き起こす」　(5) die down「(嵐・騒ぎなどが)おさまる，静まる」

3(1) make a lot of contributions to ～「～に多大な貢献をする」。contribution「貢献，寄与」は可算名詞。　(2) result in ～「～という結果に終わる」が文全体の述語動詞。discarded by bears「クマによって捨てられた」は直前の The salmon carcasses「サケの死骸」を後ろから修飾する過去分詞句。　(3) unless は「～でない限り」という意味を表す接続詞。unless they(＝the endangered species) are protected carefully「それら(＝絶滅危惧種)が注意深く保護されない限り」は if they are not protected carefully と言い換えてもほぼ同じ意味。

4(1) 場所を表す先行詞 the beautiful village by the lake のあとに非制限用法の関係副詞〈, where〉を置き，そのあとに「1週間滞在した」＝we stayed for a week を続ける。日本語につられて，文末に there を置かないように注意。　(2)「～する人はほとんどいない」を Few people ～で表す。few は「数が非常に少ない」ことを強調する。　(3) span「(ある期間)にわたる，及ぶ」を現在完了形で使う。　(4)〈the result was that S＋V〉「結果としてSがVした」。この result は「結果，結末」を表す名詞。cf. as a result「結果として」

Part 2　基本問題

1(1) abundance　(2) composition
　(3) genus　(4) natal

2(1) at sea　(2) Multiply, by

(3) vary in   (4) migrate

(5) juveniles

3 (1) have a long-term effect on the marine ecosystem

(2) After emerging from the gravel

(3) contains less than 1% of salt

4 (1)(例)She has an extraordinary musical talent.

(2)(例)A cow produces an average of 24 liters of milk per day.

(3)(例)The lizard can weigh up to 150 kilograms.

(4)(例)Even though it was raining hard, Emma kept on shopping.

解説

1 (1) abundance 名「豊富, 多量」／ abundant 形「豊富な」 (2) composed of ～「～から成る」／ composition 名「構成, 成分」。nutrient composition「栄養成分」 (3) genus 名「(生物分類の)属」／ genius 名「天才」 (4) natal 形「生まれた」／ natural 形「自然の」

2 (1) at sea「海で」 (2) multiply ～ by …「～に…をかける」 (3) vary in ～「～において異なる」 (4) migrate to ～「(場所)に渡りをする」 (5) juvenile 名「年少者, (動物の)子ども」。形として「年少者の」という意味でも用いる。

3 (1) have a long-term effect on ～で「～に長期的な影響を及ぼす」。log-term のほか, harmful「有害な」, significant「かなりの, 重大な」などの形容詞もよく使われる。 (2) emerge from ～「～から現れる」。前置詞 after のあとに～ ing(動名詞)が続く形に注意。 (3) contains less than 1% of salt で「塩分含有量が 1 パーセントに満たない」という意味。

4 (1)「音楽の才能がある」は has a musical talent で表す。extraordinary「並外れた」

は musical の前に置く。 (2)「1 日に平均～リットルの…」は an average of ～ liters of ～ per day で表す。A cow produces on average 24 liters of milk per day. または A cow produces 24 liters of milk on average per day. としても, 意味はほぼ同じ。 (3)「体重が～キログラムにもなる」は, 自動詞の weigh「重さが～ある」と up to ～「(最大)～まで」を組み合わせて, weight up to ～ kilograms で表す。 (4) even though ～は although を強調した形で,「～だが, それでも」という意味。even though のあとには〈事実〉(「雨が降っていた」など)や〈了解事項〉(「朝の通勤電車は混雑する」など)が続く。cf. even if ～「たとえ～でも」(仮定)

Part 3　基本問題

1 (1) aggressive   (2) hibernators

(3) equation   (4) reproductive

2 (1) neither, nor   (2) feed on

(3) depends on   (4) feasted on

3 (1) gave birth to a baby girl

(2) favors those that get the most nourishment

(3) a good way to improve your English

(4) deposit enough fat to survive

4 (1)(例)Oil is a crucial resource for all industries.

(2)(例)Health is closely tied to a balanced diet and sufficient sleep.

(3)(例)Starting something without plans and goals can result in a waste of time.

(4)(例)Once Jack begins studying, he concentrates on it for hours.

解説

1 (1) aggressive 形「積極的な, 攻撃的な」／ aggregate 動「集まる」 (2) hibernator 名

「冬眠動物」／ hibernation 名「冬眠」　(3) equal 形「等しい」／ equation 名「方程式」　(4) reproductive 形「繁殖の」／ reproduce 動「繁殖する」

2(1)「A することも B することもできない」は can neither *A* nor *B* で表す。この文では，助動詞 can のあとなので，*A* と *B* はどちらも動詞の原形。　(2) feed on ～「(動物などが)～を常食とする」。*cf.* live on ～「(人が)～を常食とする」　(3) depend on ～「～にかかっている，左右される」　(4) feast on ～「(特に豪華な食事)を楽しむ」

3(1) give birth to ～「～を生む」　(2) favor those that ～〉「～するものに味方する」。この favor は「～に味方する，～にとって有利に働く」という意味の動詞。those that ～ の those は漠然と「もの」を表し，このあとに関係代名詞節などの修飾語句を伴う。*cf.* those who ～「～する人々」　(3) a good way to *do*「～するのによい方法」。improve *one's* English「英語力を向上させる」　(4) deposit 動「～を蓄える」。〈enough＋名詞＋to *do*〉「～するのに十分な…」

4(1) a crucial resource for ～「～にとって極めて重要な資源」。*cf.* natural resources「天然資源」　(2)「～と密接に関わっている」を be closely tied to ～で表す。　(3) 動名詞を主語にして，「～に終わる」を result in ～で表す。result from ～「～に起因する」と混同しないように注意。「時間の無駄」は a waste of time で，a が必要。　(4)「ひとたび～すると」を表す接続詞は once。concentrate on ～「～に集中する」は重要熟語。

Part 4　基本問題

1(1) selectively　(2) density
　(3) scavenging　(4) decomposed
2(1) a bite　(2) flushed out

(3) After all　(4) would, otherwise
3(1) has made fresh water available
　(2) with most of the seats not occupied
　(3) far more food than they can eat
4(1)(例)In the past, it was common for Japanese people to eat rice for breakfast.
　(2)(例)Old cars consume more gasoline compared to modern cars.〔別解〕Compared to modern cars, old cars consume more gasoline.
　(3)(例)It took him less than an hour to set up his computer.

解説

1(1) selectively 副「選んで，選択的に」／ selective 形「選択的な」　(2) density 名「密度」／ dense 形「密の，(霧などが)濃い」　(3) scavenging ＜ scavenge 動「(ごみなど)をあさる」／ scavenger 名「清掃動物・昆虫(生態系において，死骸などをあさる動物・昆虫)」　(4) decomposed 形「腐敗した」／ decompose 動「腐敗する，腐敗させる」

2(1) eat a bite「一口食べる」という意味の熟語。without eating a bite of ～で「～を一口も食べずに」となる。　(2) flush ～ out「(水などが)～を押し流す」の受け身形。　(3) after all「結局のところ，しょせんは」　(4) otherwise「それなしには」に〈仮定〉が込められた仮定法過去。otherwise は副詞なので，助動詞 would not と本動詞 be の間に置かれる。空所直前の that は，easy access to the internet を先行詞とする関係代名詞。

3(1)〈make＋O＋C〉「O を C にする」の基本文型。make ～ available for … で「～を…に利用可能にする」という意味。　(2)〈with＋O＋過去分詞〉で「O が～された状態で」という〈付帯状況〉を表す。not occupied は「(座席に)人が座っていない」状態を表し，unoccupied

と交換可能。　(3)〈far more＋名詞〉で「はるかに多くの〜」という比較の強調になる。than のあとに〈S＋V〉＝they can eat が続くことに注意。

4 (1)「以前は」＝in the past は文頭に置き，〈it is＋形容詞＋for 人＋to *do*〉「…することは人にとって〜である」の形式主語構文を続ける。　(2)「〜を消費する」は consume で表す。分詞構文の compared to 〜「〜と比較して」は文頭に置くこともできるが，その場合は主節との間にカンマが必要となる。　(3)「人が〜するのに時間が…かかる」は〈It takes＋O（人）＋O（時間）＋to *do*〉の構文で表す。「1時間もかからなかった」は「1時間未満かかった」と考えて，O（時間）の位置に less than an hour を置く。

発展問題

(1) rainforests

(2) 赤道と極地方の間／熱帯よりもはるかに穏やか／年間を通じて降雨量がかなり多い

(3) ほかの捕食動物からの邪魔を受けずに食べようとして，捕らえたサケを森に持ち込む（38字）

(4) the entire Earth consists of one large ecosystem made up of smaller ones

(5) ウ，エ

解説

(1) 下線部①の those は，直前に出てきた複数名詞の繰り返しを避けるために用いられる代名詞で，ここでは同じ文の rainforests「雨林」を指す。なお，rainforests だけで「熱帯雨林」を指すこともあるが，本文では「熱帯雨林」tropical rainforests と「温帯雨林」temperate rainforests を区別して用いている。

(2) 第2段落第1〜2文の内容と合うように，語注も参考にしながら，空所に日本語を補う。

第1文に出てくる polar regions「極地方」とは，南緯66度50分より南の「南極圏」と，北緯66度34分より北の「北極圏」の両方をまとめて指す言い方。関係副詞 where の先行詞は the mid-latitudes「中緯度地方」。第2文後半では，温帯雨林の特徴として，「年間を通じて降雨量がかなり多い」ことを述べている。

(3) 第3段落の下線部③は「このようにして，産卵期のサケは死後も森の生態系に貢献し続けている」という意味。In this way は，直前の内容を集約するつなぎ語句なので，これよりも前の第5〜6文から答えを探す。サケを捕まえたあとに捕食動物がとりやすい行動について述べているのは，第5文である。they have caught は the salmon を先行詞とする関係代名詞節。捕食動物が川で捕ったサケを森林に持ち込む目的は，to eat 以下に述べられている。without interference from 〜は「〜からの邪魔を受けずに」という意味。

(4) 下線部④の the idea とは，具体的には第4段落第3文の that 以下，つまり「地球全体が小さな生態系の集まりからなるひとつの大きな生態系である」という考え方を指している。smaller ones＝smaller ecosystems。

(5) ア　選択肢の訳「これまでに発見された世界の生物種の約80パーセントが温帯雨林に生息していると推定されている」　第1段落第2文によれば，「全世界で確認されている生物種の約80パーセントが生息している」のは熱帯雨林であって，温帯雨林ではない。従って，選択肢アは誤り。　イ　選択肢の訳「グレート・ベア・レインフォレストは地球上最大の熱帯雨林の1つである」　第2段落第3文によれば，「グレート・ベア・レインフォレストは世界最大の温帯雨林」なので，選択肢イは誤り。　ウ　選択肢の訳「温帯雨林は，熱帯雨林と同様，地球の気候を調整す

る働きをしている」　第1段落第3文，および第4文によれば，熱帯雨林と温帯雨林のどちらも「地球の気候を調節する」(regulating the global climate)働きを持っていることがわかる。従って，これが正解の1つ目。　エ 選択肢の訳 「グレート・ベア・レインフォレストの生態系は産卵のために遡上するサケに大きく依存している」　第2段落第4文で，グレート・ベア・レインフォレストの生態系について，「何千年もの間，産卵のために遡上するサケに依存してきた」(has relied on spawning salmon for its vitality for thousands of years)と述べている内容と一致。これが正解の2つ目。　オ 選択肢の訳 「グレート・ベア・レインフォレストは地球上の生態系がそれぞれ独立して存在していることを示している」　第4段落第1～2文に，「地球上の生態系は複雑，かつ予想もしない形で互いにつながって」おり，どの生態系も「単独で存在することはできない」(cannot exist alone)とある。従って，選択肢オは誤り。

<全訳>
グレート・ベア・レインフォレスト
　「雨林」(rainforests)という単語から，あなたは赤道に近い熱帯地域に存在する①ものを思い浮かべるかもしれない。熱帯雨林は生物多様性のホットスポットであり，そこには全世界で確認されている生物種の約80パーセントが生息していると考えられている。それだけでない。熱帯雨林は大量の二酸化炭素を隔離し，蒸発散と呼ばれるプロセスを通じて水分を放出することによって，地球の気候を調整する上で極めて重要な役割を果たしている。しかし，「温帯雨林」と呼ばれる別の種類の熱帯雨林について知っている人はそれほど多くはない。温帯雨林もまた，地球の気候を調整する上で重要な役割を果たしているのである。
　②温帯雨林は赤道と極地方の間の中緯度地方に位置し，その気温は熱帯よりもはるかに穏やかである。温帯雨林は主に海岸沿いの山岳地帯に分布しており，こうした地理的条件のために，年間を通じてかなりの降雨量がある。カナダのブリティッシュ・コロンビア州の太平洋岸にあるグ

レート・ベア・レインフォレスト(Great Bear Rainforest)は，世界最大の沿岸温帯雨林である。生態学的観点から見ると，グレート・ベア・レインフォレストはとりわけ重要である。なぜならその生態系は何千年もの間，産卵のために遡上するサケに依存してきたからである。
　グレート・ベア・レインフォレストには2千以上の小川や河川があり，熱帯雨林全体をつなぐ水路網として機能している。さらに，これらの小川や河川は，パシフィック・サーモンに不可欠な産卵場所を提供している。毎年，何百万匹ものパシフィック・サーモンが産卵のためにこの水域に戻ってくる。これら産卵期のサケは，クマ，オオカミ，ワシなど熱帯雨林に生息する多くの動物種の貴重な食料源となっている。こうした捕食動物は，ほかの捕食動物からの邪魔を受けずに食べようとして，捕らえたサケを森に持ち込むことが多い。森に放置されたサケの死骸は，しばしば死肉をあさる動物や昆虫に食べられ，分解されて森の肥料となる。③このようにして，産卵のために遡上するサケは，死後も森の生態系に貢献し続けているのである。
　グレート・ベア・レインフォレストは，地球上の生態系がいかに複雑に，そして予想もしない形で互いにつながっているかを教えてくれる。どの生態系も独自の特徴を持っているが，単独で存在することはできない。環境保護への取り組みは，地球全体が小さな生態系の集まりからなるひとつの大きな生態系であるという④考え方に基づくべきである。

Lesson 3　(pp.16-21)
Child Labor Problems in the Ivory Coast Cocoa Sector

Part 1　基本問題

1(1) producer　　(2) inland
　(3) crackdown　　(4) publicized

2(1) picked up　　(2) youngsters
　(3) skinny, wringing
　(4) mounting demands

3(1) are free of any harmful chemicals
　(2) referred to as the heartland of America
　(3) were forced to work on the cocoa plantation

4(1)(例)Some consumers choose to buy ethical products.
　(2)(例)Many students are involved in volunteering activities to help their

communities.

(3)(例)The Ivory Coast is known as a producer of high-quality cocoa beans.

(4)(例)Child labor is commonly practiced in certain developing countries.

解説

■1 (1) producer 名「生産者，生産国」／ production 名「生産，製造」 (2) inland 形「内陸の」／ indoors 副「室内で，屋内で」 (3) crackup 名「衝突」／ crackdown 名「取り締まり」 (4) publicized < publicize 動「公表する，公に宣言する」／ public 形「公の，公共の」

■2 (1) pick up「～を連行する」 (2) youngster「若者」 (3) skinny「やせこけた」，wring one's hands「手をもみ合わせる」 (4) mounting demands from ～「～からの増える一方の要求」

■3 (1) be free of ～「～がない，～を含んでいない」 (2) refer to A as B「A を B と呼ぶ」の受け身形は A is referred to as B。 (3) be forced to do「～するように強制される，～せざるを得ない」

■4 (1) ethical「倫理的な」 (2) be involved in ～「～に参加する，～にかかわる」 (3) be known as ～「～として知られている」 (4)「児童労働」＝child labor を主語にする。

Part 2　基本問題

■1 (1) rider (2) convoy (3) swoop

■2 (1) mobilized (2) left, with
(3) able to (4) heap of (5) precede

■3 (1) was presented as the guest of honor
(2) were seen roaming the streets
(3) If this is the case for you

■4 (1)(例)The factory produces various products made from natural rubber.
(2)(例)Masato commutes to work every day by motorcycle.

(3)(例)Mina bought a dozen eggs at the supermarket.

(4)(例)The doll museum is the only museum of its kind in Japan.

解説

■1 (1) rider 名「(オートバイなどに)乗る人」／ riding 名「(オートバイなどに)乗ること」 (2) convey 動「～を運ぶ」／ convoy 名「車両集団」 (3) swoop 名「急襲」／ hamlet 名「(小さな)村」

■2 (1) mobilize 動「～を動員する」 (2) leave A with B「A を B に預ける」 (3) 過去のある特定の時に「(一時的に)～することができた」という場合は，was able to do を用いる。could は不可。 (4) the heap of laundry「洗濯物の山」 (5) precede 動「～に先行する，先んじる」 cf. unprecedented 形「前例のない」

■3 (1) be presented as ～「～として紹介される」 (2)〈see＋O＋現在分詞〉「O が～しているのを見る」の受け身形は，元の O を主語にして〈be 動詞＋seen＋現在分詞〉の形にする。 (3) If this is the case for you で「その場合は」という決まった言い方。

■4 (1)「天然ゴムを原料にした」＝made from natural rubber を various products のあとに置く。 (2)「バイクで通勤する」は commute to work by motorcycle で表す。 (3)「1 ダースの～」は，現在では〈a dozen＋名詞の複数形〉で表す。cf. two dozen eggs「2 ダースの卵」 (4)「このような種類の，この種の」は of its kind で表す。

Part 3　基本問題

■1 (1) reception (2) countryside
(3) psychologists (4) enrollment

■2 (1) take in (2) pick, up
(3) fight against (4) Apart from

3(1) is being carried out by

(2) taught her the skill of sewing

(3) made it his trade

4(1)(例)In some countries, a significant number of adults are illiterate.

(2)(例)Many cases of child abuse are reported every year.

(3)(例)They were told to take a break after two hours' work.

(4)(例)It is often difficult to understand the psychology of adolescents.

解説

1 (1) receive 動「～を受け入れる」／reception 名「受付」 (2) countryside 名「田園地帯, 田舎」／countrywide 形副「全国的な[に]」 (3) psychologist 名「心理学者」／psychological 形「心理学上の, 心理的な」 (4) enroll 動「入学する, 登録する」／enrollment 名「入学, 登録」

2(1) take in「～を引き取る, 受け入れる, (栄養など)を摂取する」 (2) pick up「～を迎えに来る[行く]」 (3) in the fight against ～「～に対する闘いにおいて」。*cf.* fight against ～「～を相手に闘う」 (4) apart from ～「～は別にして, ～以外に」

3(1)〈be 動詞＋being＋過去分詞〉は現在進行形の受動態で,「～されているところだ」という意味を表す。by 以下が動作主。 (2)〈teach＋O₁＋O₂〉「O₁(人)に O₂(もの)を教える」。 (3) made it(＝gardening) his trade「それ(＝造園[園芸])を職業にした」と考える。〈make＋O＋C〉「O を C にする」

4(1)「かなりの多くの数の～」は a significant number of ～,「読み書きができない」は illiterate で表す。 (2) many cases of ～「多くの～の事例」 (3) after two hours' work「2時間働いたあとで」の所有格 hours'(名詞の複数形＋アポストロフィー)に注意。 (4)〈It

is＋形容詞＋to 不定詞〉の形式主語構文で表す。

Part 4　基本問題

1(1) enslaved　　(2) surveillance

(3) legal

2(1) sentenced, to　(2) convicted, trafficking

(3) below, poverty line

(4) subsist on

(5) prosecutor, imprisonment

3(1) More than half of the students

(2) was brought to court

(3) has been conducted since 2010

4(1)(例)The course aims at improving students' presentation skills.

(2)(例)Drinking by minors is prohibited by law.

(3)(例)The boy was punished for telling a lie.

(4)(例)Many small companies give up buying new computers because they can't afford them.

解説

1(1) enslaved ＜ enslave 動「～を奴隷にする」／slavery 名「奴隷制度」 (2) surveillance 名「監視, 監督」／oversee 動「～を監督する」 (3) legal 形「法的な, 法律上の」／legally 副「法的に, 法律上は」

2(1)〈sentence＋O(人)＋to ～〉「人に(判決)を言い渡す」 (2) be convicted of ～「～の罪で有罪判決を受ける」 (3) live below the poverty line「貧困ラインを下回る生活を送る」 (4) subsist on ～「～で生計を立てている」 (5) the prosecutor「検察(側)」 imprisonment「懲役(刑)」

3(1) more than half of ～「～の半数以上」 (2) bring ～ to court「～を法廷に持ち込む」の受け身形。 (3)〈have[has] been＋過去分詞〉

は受動態の現在完了形。ここでは〈継続〉。

4 (1) aim at ～ing「～することを目的にしている」 (2)「～は法律で禁止されている」は be prohibited by law で表す。 (3) be punished for ～ing「～したために罰を受ける」 (4) give up ～ing「～することをあきらめる」。can't afford ～「～の経済的余裕がない」

発展問題

(1) ア

(2) 西アフリカの2つの国／世界のカカオ生産量の半分以上

(3) proper amounts of rain for cocoa trees to grow normally（10語）／cocoa trees' ability to fight diseases and pests（8語）

(4) decline

(5) イ，オ

解説

(1)「新興国においても」となるように，アの as well「～もまた」を選ぶ。

(2) 下線部②の That は，直前の第2段落第5～6文の内容，つまり「コートジボワールとガーナという西アフリカの2大カカオ生産国だけで世界のカカオ生産量の半分以上を占めている」ことを指している。account for ～は「（割合が）～を占める」という意味。

(3) 第3段落第2～3文から，指定された語数で答えを探す。for cocoa trees は不定詞句 to grow normally の意味上の主語。to make matters worse「さらに悪いことに」は，好ましくない事例を追加するときに用いるディスコース・マーカー（談話標識）。

(4) 第2段落第7文に a minor decline in cocoa harvest「カカオの収穫量がわずかに減ること」とある。

(5) ア 選択肢の訳「インドと中国は，チョコレート需要の増加に対応するため，カカオ豆の生産を検討中である」 第1段落では，インド

と中国におけるチョコレートの需要の増加について述べているが，自国での栽培については何も述べていない。 イ 選択肢の訳「世界のカカオ市場は，熱帯地域の2つの発展途上国の収穫量減少の影響を受けやすい」 第2段落第5～7文の内容と一致。コートジボワールとガーナの2国だけで世界のカカオ生産量の半分以上を占めているため，その収穫量がわずかに減るだけでカカオ市場に大きな影響が出る可能性があると述べている。 ウ 選択肢の訳「世界最大のカカオ生産国は南米にあるが，それはその地域の気候がカカオの木を育てるのに最適だからである」 第2段落第3文から，南米においてもカカオの木が栽培されていることがわかるが，世界最大の生産国は南米ではなく西アフリカにあるので，誤り。 エ 選択肢の訳「一部のカカオ農家は，カカオの木に悪影響を及ぼす病害虫に対処するため，科学者に支援を求めている」 第3段落でカカオの木に悪影響を及ぼす病害虫について述べているが，科学者の支援については何も記述がない。 オ 選択肢の訳「気候変動の影響をより受けやすくなっているため，多くのカカオ農園ではカカオの木の栽培を断念している」 第3段落第1～3文の内容と一致。地球規模の気候変動のためにカカオの木が正常に育たなくなり，多くの生産農家がカカオの栽培を断念していることがわかる。これが正解の2つ目。

<全訳>
伸び続けるカカオの需要
　チョコレートの世界的な需要が急速に伸びている。チョコレートは主に先進国で消費され，甘いものを食べてリラックスしたい人々に愛されている。近年では，新興国において①もチョコレートの消費が急速に増えている。特にインドや中国では，特別なひとときのためにチョコレートをよく食べる人が増えており，チョコレート市場が急成長

している。

　問題は，チョコレート製造における主な原料のひとつとなるカカオ豆が地球上のどこでも自然に育つわけではないということである。カカオの木が順調に育つためには，暑く湿潤な気候と十分な降雨量が必要である。そのため，カカオの木は，赤道をはさんで北緯20度から南緯20度の範囲の熱帯地域でだけ栽培されている。しばしば「カカオベルト」と呼ばれるこの地域は，中央アフリカおよび西アフリカからインドネシア，そして中南米まで及ぶ。実際，世界のカカオの90パーセント以上は，これらの地域に位置する発展途上国において生産されている。特にコートジボワールとガーナは世界の2大カカオ生産国である。これら2つの西アフリカの国だけで世界のカカオ生産量の半分以上を占めている。②そのため，これら2つの国におけるカカオの収穫量がわずかに減るだけで，世界のカカオ市場に大きな影響を及ぼす可能性がある。

　③近年，多くのカカオ農家がカカオの木の栽培を断念せざるを得ない状況にある。地球規模の気候変動のために，多くのカカオ生産国では，カカオの木が正常に育つのに適した降雨量が得られていない。さらに悪いことには，気候変動が続く中で，カカオの木の病気や害虫に対する抵抗力が弱まっている。その結果，多くのカカオの木が枯れ，カカオの生産が④減少しているのである。

　このような危機的な状況に直面していても，多くのカカオ農家には効果的な対策を講じるだけの経済的余裕がない。世界の代表的なチョコレートメーカーのいくつかは，カカオ農園を保護し，カカオの生産を回復させるためのプロジェクトに取り組んでいる。しかし，チョコレートの需要が増加するペースは，こうした新たな取り組みが進むペースを上回っているのが現状である。

Lesson 4 　　(pp.22-27)
Foreign Residents in Japan

Part 1　基本問題

1(1) rejuvenate　(2) immigration
　(3) objective　(4) succession

2(1) ranks fourth　(2) followed by
　(3) technical intern trainee　(4) In terms

3(1) is regarded not as a singer but as
　(2) The statistics show how many hours
　(3) is less than half of that

4(1)(例)In Japanese schools, students are

---

expected to clean their classrooms every day.

(2)(例)Many countries are facing a declining birthrate.

(3)(例)It is argued that eating modest amounts of chocolate is good for your health.

(4)(例)The rain prevented us from going cycling.

解説

1(1) rejuvenate 動「～を回復させる，活性化する」／ juvenile 名形「未成年者(の)」　(2) immigration 名「入国，移民」／ immigrant 名「(外国からの)移民」　(3) objective 名「目的」／ objection 名「反論，異議」　(4) succeed 動「継承する」／ succession 名「継承」

2(1)〈rank＋助数詞〉「～位に入る」　(2) followed by ～「そのあとに～が続く」　(3) technical intern trainee「技能実習生」　(4) in terms of ～「～に関して言えば」

3(1) be regarded not as A but as B「AではなくBとみなされる」　(2) statistics 名「統計，統計学」　(3) less than half of ～「～の半分ほどもない」。代名詞の that は the number of schools の代わり。

4(1) be expected to do「～するよう期待されている」は〈expect＋O＋to do〉の受け身形。　(2) face a declining birthrate「出生率の低下に直面する」　(3) It is argued that ...「…と主張されている」。「適量の～」は modest amounts of ～で表す。　(4)〈prevent＋O＋from ～ing〉「Oが～するのを妨げる」で表す。

Part 2　基本問題

1(1) utilize　(2) Except for
　(3) socialize

2(1) known as　(2) large amounts

(3) put up　　　　　(4) ample budget

(5) vicinity of

3(1) move to big cities for higher wages

(2) paid some money to intermediary agencies

(3) enough money to clear off all his debt

4(1)(例)The boy saved as much money as possible to buy a baseball glove.

(2)(例)My grandfather seldom leaves his house because of his old age.

(3)(例)Every year, many tourists come over to Japan to experience its traditional culture.

(4)(例)The facility houses not only a museum but also a theater.

解説

1(1) utilize 動「〜を利用する」／ utility 名「実用性，役に立つもの」 (2) except for 〜と except はどちらも「〜を除いて」の意味だが，文頭に置くときは必ず except for 〜を用いる。 (3) social 形「社交的な，社交上の」／ socialize 動「(社交上)付き合う」

2(1) be known as 〜「〜として知られる」 *cf.* be known for 〜「〜で知られる」, be known to 〜「〜に知られる」 (2) large amounts of 〜「大量の〜」。of のあとには不可算名詞が続く。 (3) put up「〜を建てる」(≒build, construct) (4) ample budget「潤沢な予算」 (5) in the vicinity of 〜「〜の近くに」

3(1) move to 〜 for higher wages「より高い賃金を求めて〜に行く」 (2) pay some money to intermediary agencies for a work permit「労働許可証を得るために仲介業者にお金を払う」 (3) clear off all *one's* debt「借金を完済する」

4(1)「できるだけたくさんの〜」は as much 〜 as possible で表す。 (2) seldom 副「めったに〜ない」 (3) come over to 〜「〜にやって

来る」 (4)〈not only A but also B〉「A だけでなく B もまた」。

Part 3　基本問題

1(1) representatives　(2) laborers

(3) fee

2(1) newcomer　　　(2) composed of

(3) settle into　　(4) suffer from

(5) divided, into

3(1) take getting clean water as a matter of course

(2) insisted on going shopping

(3) are struggling hard to learn

4(1)(例)They failed to find any common ground in their discussion.

(2)(例)Mutual understanding is necessary between teammates.

(3)(例)As for me, I'm always trying to choose environmentally-friendly products.

(4)(例)They got over their cultural differences as they spent more time together.

解説

1(1) represent 動「〜を代表する」／ representative 名「代表」 (2) labor 名「労働」／ laborer 名「労働者」。ただし, labor は the labor の形で，集合的に「労働者(たち)」を表す。 (3) fee 名「(入場・参加に必要な)料金」。membership fee は「会費」。fare 名は「(交通機関の)料金, 運賃」に用いる語。

2(1) newcomer 名「新しく来た人, 新人」 (2) be composed of 〜「〜で構成されている」 (3) settle into 〜「(住まいなど)に落ち着く, 定住する」 (4) suffer from 〜「(病気)を患う, (問題などに)悩まされる, 苦しむ」 (5) divide 〜 into …「〜を…に分ける,分割する」

3(1) take 〜 as a matter of course「〜を当然

15

のことと考える」。ここでは「〜」の位置に動名詞が置かれている。　(2) insist on 〜ing「〜すると言ってきかない[言い張る]」　(3) struggle hard to *do*「〜しようと奮闘努力する」

4(1) find any common ground in 〜「〜に何か１つでも合意点[一致点]を見出す」。fail to *do*「〜できない，〜し損なう」　(2) mutual understanding「相互理解」。クラスメイトは通例３人以上であるが，「二者の間で相互に」の意味では，among ではなく between を用いる。　(3) as for 〜「〜に関して言えば」　(4) get over *one's* cultural differences「(お互いの)文化の相違を乗り越える」

Part 4　基本問題

1(1) status　　　　(2) terms
　(3) or
2(1) for, sake
　(2) regardless of nationality
　(3) more than　　(4) in reality
　(5) be amended
3(1) enables users to edit digital images
　(2) make it possible to go
　(3) expand the acceptance quota for new students
4(1)(例)Yuki is going to get married to Kaito next month.
　(2)(例)The library allows you to borrow up to three books at one time.
　(3)(例)The family chose to make a permanent home in Japan.
　(4)(例)Climate change is expected to affect food production around the world.

解説

1(1) status 名「状態，立場，地位」／ statue 名「彫像」　(2) terms of the contract「契約条件」。この場合，term は必ず複数形で用いる。
　(3) choose either chicken or pork「チキンか

ポークのどちらかを選ぶ」

2(1) for 〜's sake「〜 のために 」　(2) regardless of nationality「国籍に関係なく」　(3)〈no more than＋数量〉「わずか〜，たった〜」(≒only 〜)　(4) in reality「実際には，現実には」　(5) amend 動「(法律など)を改正する，修正する」

3(1)〈enable＋O＋to *do*〉「O が〜することを可能にする」　(2) make it possible to *do*「〜することを可能にする」。形式目的語の it は to 不定詞の内容を受ける。　(3) expand the acceptance quota「受け入れ枠を拡大する」。quota 名「割当量，定員，定数」

4(1) get married to 〜「〜と結婚する」　(2)〈allow＋O＋to *do*〉「O に〜することを認める」。up to 〜は，「最大[最高]〜まで」という〈数量の上限〉を表す。　(3)「〜に永住する」は make a permanent home in 〜で表す。　(4) be expected to *do*「〜することが予想される」

発展問題

(1) adapt to the customs and traditions of the local people
(2) 同じ国からやって来た人々が外国においても集まって，独自のコミュニティを形成する
(3) イ
(4) ウ
(5) ウ，エ

解説

(1) 第１段落第２文の This saying emphasizes that …の that 節で，when we are in a foreign land, we should …「異国の地にいるときは，…すべきである」と述べているので，この we should のあとに続く10語を抜き出す。adapt to 〜「〜に適応する」は，最終段落第５文にも出てくる重要表現である。

(2) 第2段落第1文で，'When in Rome, do as the Romans do.' ということわざとは逆に，実際には，異国の地においても同じ国の出身者は固まりやすく，独自のコミュニティを形成する傾向があることを述べている。

(3) These barriers は，直前の文の language barriers を指す。「言語の障壁は外国人労働者が日本人の同僚や，住居，オフィス，工場の近くに住む地域住民と◻◻◻することを妨げる」という文脈から，イの interacting with ～「～と交流すること」を選ぶ。

(4) 補う英文は，「それは彼らが言語の障壁を乗り越えることを可能にする」という意味。主語 It，および them が何を指すかを考えながら位置を選ぶ。ウの位置に入れると，It は working together to find common ground を，them は people from different places を指すことになり，文脈が通る。

(5) ア 選択肢の訳 「この古いことわざは，古代ローマの人々がお互いを尊重しながら暮らしていたことを私たちに教えてくれる」 第1段落第2文の説明と矛盾。 イ 選択肢の訳 「チャイナタウンは，人々がその土地の習慣にいかによく適応できるかを示すよい例である」 第2段落に出てくる Chinatowns は，同じ国の出身者が異国の地で作った独自のコミュニティの例として挙げられているので，これは誤り。 ウ 選択肢の訳 「同じ国籍の人々は外国でも独自のコミュニティをしばしば形成する」 第2段落第1文の主旨と一致。これが正解の1つ目。 エ 選択肢の訳 「すべての外国人労働者が日本人の同僚や現地の人々とうまくやっているわけではない」 第3段落第3～5文の主旨と一致。これが正解の2つ目。 オ 選択肢の訳 「日本で仕事を得るためには，外国人労働者は日本語でのコミュニケーション能力を身につける必要がある」 第4段落最終文の内容と矛盾。日本語でコミュニケーションを交わす能力については特に触れていない。

<全訳>
「郷に入っては」

　「郷に入っては郷に従え」ということわざがある。このことわざは，異国の地にいるときは，現地の人々の習慣や伝統に適応すべきであることを強調している。その起源は，紀元4世紀のローマ帝国時代にまでさかのぼることができる。現在でも，「郷に入っては」（When in Rome）と言うだけで，①その意味が伝わるほど，このことわざは広く知られている。しかし，本当に難しいのは，そのアドバイスを実践することにあるのだ。

　現実には，同じ国からやって来た人々は，外国においても集まって，独自のコミュニティを形成することが多い。例えば，チャイナタウンやコリアンタウンは世界各地に見られる。同じように，海外で暮らす日本人は，地元の人たちと交流せずに，日本人同士で固まる傾向がある。デジタル時代の現代においては，このような「群がる」パターンはさらに助長される可能性がある。②こうした傾向の大きな要因の1つは言語の障壁である。

　近年では，かなりの数の外国人がさまざまな分野において仕事を見つけたり，技能を習得したりするために日本にやって来る。人手不足に悩む日本にとって，彼らは貴重な人的資源となることが期待されている。しかしながら，外国人労働者を受け入れる職場では，言語の障壁による相互理解のギャップに直面することが多い。この障壁のために，外国人労働者は日本人の同僚や，住居，オフィス，工場の近くに住む地域住民③と交流することができない。また，日本の習慣に従わない外国人労働者もおり，彼らは自分たちだけでグループを作り，自分たちのスタイルを通すようになる。

　出生率の低下が進んでいることを考えると，日本は今後ますます外国人労働者に頼らざるを得なくなっていくことだろう。職場での相互理解には効果的なコミュニケーションが不可欠であり，言語はその中核を成すものである。その一方で，異なる土地から来た人たちは，共通点を見つけるために協力し合うことによって，お互いをより深く理解できるようになる。④このようにして，彼らは言語の障壁を乗り越えることが可能となる。受け入れ側にとっては，外国人労働者が日本の習慣や伝統に適応しながら，自分の得意なことを発揮できる環境を提供することが非常に重要である。一方，外国人労働者は，日本のルールや習慣を理解し，それに従うよう意識的に努力する必要があると言えるだろう。

17

Lesson 5　(pp.28-33)
The Edible Schoolyard

Part 1　基本問題

1 (1) charismatic　(2) wholly
(3) visionary　(4) edible

2 (1) curriculum　(2) harvested
(3) planted, seeds　(4) mission
(5) ecological

3 (1) beautified her room with a lot of flowers
(2) involved the students in an interesting experiment
(3) realize the way daily food affects

4 (1)(例)The zoo is a place in which you can see various kinds of animals.
(2)(例)Paul reads books on his way to and from work.
(3)(例)Jane felt dismay at her parents' reaction to her future plans.
(4)(例)Some people listen to music before going to bed so that they can sleep well.

解説
1 (1) charismatic 形「カリスマ性のある」／ charisma 名「カリスマ」　(2) whole 形名「全体(の)」／ wholly 副「すっかり，もっぱら」
(3) visionary 名「ビジョンを持った人」／ vision 名「ビジョン」　(4) endurable 形「耐えられる」／ edible 形「食べられる，食用の」 cf. edible flowers「食用の花」

2 (1) curriculum「カリキュラム」。綴りに注意。
(2) harvest 動「〜を収穫する」。名として「収穫物」の意味でも用いる。　(3) plant seeds「種をまく」　(4) mission 名「使命，ミッション」　(5) ecological 形「生態学の，環境上の」。名詞形は ecology「生態学，エコロジー」

3 (1) beautify 〜 with …「〜を…で美しくする」
(2) involve 〜 in …「〜を…に巻き込む[参加

させる]」　(3)〈the way S＋V〉「いかに S が V するか」

4 (1)「動物園はその中でいろいろな種類の動物を見ることができる場所です」と考えて，先行詞 place のあとに in which(前置詞＋関係代名詞)を続ける。　(2) on one's way to and from work「仕事の行き帰りに」。cf. on one's way to and from school「学校の行き帰りに」
(3) feel dismay at 〜「〜にうろたえる，狼狽する」。「〜に対する反応」は reaction to 〜で表す。　(4) Some people を主語にする。「よく眠れるように」は〈so that S can V〉「S が V できるように」で表す。

Part 2　基本問題

1 (1) germinates　(2) refurbished
(3) inspiration

2 (1) ugly　(2) tore up
(3) embedded in　(4) cleanse
(5) instilled, passion

3 (1) The company has remained a major sponsor
(2) The grant allowed the school to purchase
(3) without the schedule being affected

4 (1)(例)Each of us should play our part in realizing a sustainable society.
(2)(例)The success of a project depends on many different factors.
(3)(例)The city is looking for a way to utilize the unused facilities.
(4)(例)Asphalt roads can be built [constructed] easily and quickly.

解説
1 (1) germinate 動「発芽する」／ generate 動「〜を生む」　(2) 未来形の受動態〈will be＋過去分詞〉「〜されるだろう」の形になるように refurbished を選ぶ。　(3) inspiring 形「霊感

18

を与える」／inspiration 名「霊感，インスピ
レーション」

2(1) ugly「(外見が)醜い，見苦しい」 (2) tore
up < tear up「～を引き裂く」。動詞 tear は
tear － tore － torn と不規則変化する。 (3)
be embedded in ～「～に埋め込まれる」 (4)
cleanse ～ of …「～から…を洗い流す」 (5)
instill 動「～を教え込む，植え付ける」。
passion 名「情熱」

3(1) remain「(依然として)～のままである」は
〈S＋V＋C(名詞・形容詞・分詞)〉の文型を作
る。 (2) 無生物の grant 名「補助金」を主語
にして，〈allow＋O＋to do〉「O が～すること
を許す」の構文に組み立てる。 (3)〈without
＋O＋being＋過去分詞〉「O が～された状態
で」。without 以下は，「計画が事故の影響を
受けることなく」という意味。

4(1) play one's part「自分の役割を果たす」。主
語が each of us の場合，代名詞は所有格なら
our，目的格なら us で受ける。 (2) 一般的
な事柄をのべているので，The success of a
project を主語にする。depend on ～「～に
依存する，左右される」。 (3)「～する方法
を探している」は look for a way を現在進行
形で使う。unused 形「使われていない」 (4)
asphalt「アスファルト」の綴りに注意。

Part 3　基本問題

1(1) hands-on　　　(2) mustard
　(3) output　　　　(4) compost

2(1) right off　　　(2) without being
　(3) deer　　　　　(4) munched on

3(1) were out playing in the park
　(2) Eating what tastes good
　(3) There is no reason we should

4(1)(例)All the students are encouraged to
　　　　learn a foreign language other than
　　　　English.

(2)(例)I'm good friends with a boy whose
　　　　mother calls him Kyon.

(3)(例)Stop wasting your valuable time on
　　　　trivial things.

(4)(例)Kyoto was the first place Emma
　　　　visited while (she was) traveling in
　　　　Japan.

解説

1(1) hands-on 形「手で触れることができる，
実践的な」。× hand-on という単語は存在し
ない。 (2) mustard 名「マスタード，から
し」の綴りに注意。 (3) output 名「生産高」
／ outcome 名「結果」 (4) compost 動「～を
堆肥にする」／ compose 動「～を構成する」

2(1) right off the shelves「棚から直接」 (2) 受
動態の動名詞を用いて without being noticed
「気付かれずに」とする。 (3) deer 名「シカ」
は単複同形。cf. a deer「シカ1頭」／ a herd
of deer「シカの群れ」 (4) munch on ～「～
をむしゃむしゃ食べる」

3(1) be 動詞のあとに out 副「外へ，外出して」
を続け，そのあとに現在分詞を続ける。 (2)
what tastes good「おいしいもの」の what
は関係代名詞。 (3) There is no reason we
should「～しなくてはならない理由はない」。
reason のあとに関係副詞の why を補って考
える。

4(1) be encouraged to do「～するように奨励
される」を用いる。「～のほかに」は other than
～で表す。 (2)「その母親が彼のことを～と
呼ぶ」と考えて，所有格関係代名詞 whose を
使って表す。be good friends with ～「～と
仲よしである」の複数形 friends に注意。 (3)
「～するのをやめる」は stop ～ ing，「～を…
に無駄に費やす」は waste ～ on … で表す。
(4)〈the first place＋S＋V(過去形)〉「最初に
S が V した場所」。while she was traveling
の she was は，主節 Emma visited と同じ主

語と be 動詞なので，省略できる。

Part 4　基本問題

1 (1) nutritious　　(2) ingredients
　(3) strategy

2 (1) sessions　　(2) on, run
　(3) brought, into　　(4) At first

3 (1) see if plants grow faster with sunlight
　(2) were incorporated into the new product
　(3) seduces anyone into trying them

4 (1)(例)Most families have to manage a household on a limited budget.
　(2)(例)We spread a new tablecloth on the table before having dinner.
　(3)(例)Do you know any good recipes to beat the hot summer?
　(4)(例)Kazuo is used to waking up early in the morning.

解説

1 (1) nutrition 名「栄養」／ nutritious 形「栄養のある」　(2) ingredient 名「食材」。like ～「～のような」のあとに複数の食材が列挙されているので，複数形 ingredients を選ぶ。　(3) strategy 名「戦略，方策」／ strategic 形「戦略の，方策の」

2 (1) session 名「セッション」　(2) on the run「大急ぎで，あわてて」　(3) bring ～ into …「～を…に持ち込む」　(4) at first「最初は，当初は」。ただの First, … は「第一に」と物事を列挙する場合に用いる。

3 (1)〈see if＋S＋V〉「S が V するかどうかを確かめる」　(2) be incorporated into ～「～に盛り込まれる，組み込まれる」　(3)〈seduce＋O＋into ～ing〉「O を誘惑して～させる」

4 (1)「家計をやりくりする」は manage a household,「限られた予算で」は on a limited budget で表す。　(2)「～(の上)に…を広げる」は spread … on ～で表す。tablecloth 名

「テーブルクロス」は可算名詞。　(3) recipe 名「レシピ」の綴りに注意。「暑い夏を乗り切る」は「暑い夏を打ち負かす」と考え，beat the hot summer で表す。　(4)「～することに慣れている」は be used to ～ ing で表す。

発展問題

(1) diverse cultural and economic backgrounds
(2) 地元の市場で買った新鮮な食材
(3) the ingredients they ate
(4) 健康的で栄養価の高い食事を提供できるような自分のレストランを持つこと。(35字)
(5) ア，ウ

解説

(1) 下線部①の salad bowl「サラダボウル」とは，多様な人種・民族がそれぞれの文化・伝統の独自性を保ちながら共存しているアメリカ社会のこと。第 1 段落第 3 文の diverse cultural and economic backgrounds がこの用語の説明となっている。

(2) 第 2 段落第 4 ～ 5 文で，ウォータースがフランス留学中に体験したことを述べている。

(3) 下線部③の what to eat は「何を食べるか」という意味。同じ第 3 段落第 2 文に the ingredients they ate「彼らが食べる食材」と出てくる箇所を抜き出す。

(4) 第 3 段落第 6 文の後半(having her own … became her dream)で，フランスから帰国したウォータースが抱くようになった夢について述べている。

(5) ア　選択肢の訳「エディブル・スクールヤード・プロジェクトの目的は，生徒たちに食べ物とその産地について学ぶ機会を提供することである」　第 1 段落第 5 文の内容と一致。これが正解の 1 つ目。　イ　選択肢の訳「アリス・ウォータースは，マーティン・ルーサー・キング Jr・ミドルスクールの創立者として，エディブル・スクールヤード・プロジェクト

を支援している」　第1段落第1文の内容と不一致。アリス・ウォータースはエディブル・スクールヤード・プロジェクトを設立した人物ではあるが，マーティン・ルーサー・キングJr・ミドルスクールの創立者ではない。　ウ　選択肢の訳「大学時代にフランスに滞在したアリス・ウォータースは，人々が地元でとれた食べ物を楽しむ姿がとても好きだった」　第2段落第4～5文の主旨と一致。これが正解の2つ目。　エ　選択肢の訳「アリス・ウォータースは，忙しいアメリカ人が毎日規則正しい食事をとるためにはファーストフードが欠かせないと考えている」　第3段落第1～4文の主旨と不一致。アリス・ウォータースはファーストフードに対して批判的であった。　オ　選択肢の訳「アリス・ウォータースがバークレーに地元産の食材を使った料理を出すフランス料理店シェ・パニーズをオープンしてから，まもなく50年になる」　第4段落第2文の内容と不一致。「2021年9月に創業50年を迎えた」とある。

＜全訳＞

アリス・ウォータース

　エディブル・スクールヤード・プロジェクトは，「カリフォルニア料理」（California cuisine）で知られるローカルフード運動のパイオニア，アリス・ウォータースによって1995年に設立された。プロジェクトの最初の種がまかれた，カリフォルニア州バークレーのマーティン・ルーサー・キングJr・ミドルスクールは，①「サラダボウル」のような学習環境である。さまざまな文化的・経済的背景を持った子どもたちがこの学校に集まり，食べ物は彼らを結びつける共通言語として機能している。アリス・ウォータースは「エディブル・エデュケーション」（食べられる教育）という概念を提唱し，エディブル・スクールヤード・プロジェクトを通して，それを実践した。その目標とは，生徒が食材とその産地の関係を正しく認識できるようにすることであり，これは彼女が提唱してきたローカルフード運動の原則とも一致している。

　アリス・ウォータースのフード・ムーブメントが生まれた背景とはどのようなものなのだろうか。ウォータース自身の話として，彼女は幼い頃から味覚が鋭かったという。しかし，彼女をフード・ムーブメントへと導いたのは，②大学時代のフランス留学の経験だった。1965年にフランスに滞在していた彼女は，国内のあちこちにある家族経営の小さなレストランや，人々が毎日買い物を楽しむ地元の市場に感激した。人々は市場で買った新鮮な食材を家で調理し，家族といっしょに食べた。まだ若かったアリスにとって，それは理想的な食事の楽しみ方だった。

　当時，多くのアメリカ人は毎日大量のファーストフードを食べていた。ウォータースには，口にする食材やその調理法について，だれも気にしていないように見えた。ウォータースは，安くて不健康なファーストフードが人々の食習慣を形成し，アメリカの食文化に深く浸透していることに悲しみを覚えた。彼女は，人々は日常生活で③何を食べるかについて，もっと意識的な選択をすべきだと考えていた。当時の彼女はプロの料理人ではなかったが，ほどなくして友人を家に招き，新鮮な食材を使って，彼らのために料理を作るようになった。人に料理を振る舞うことに喜びを見出した彼女は，健康的で栄養価の高い食事を提供できるような自分のレストランを持つことが夢となった。

　④ウォータースの夢は1971年に実現した。この年，彼女はバークレーにフランス料理店「シェ・パニーズ」をオープンした。COVID-19の大流行がもたらした試練を乗り越えて，アメリカで初めて地元産の食材を使った料理を出すことをうたったこのレストランは，2021年8月に50周年を迎えた。

Lesson 6　(pp.34-39)
Restoring to Deaf People the Right to Education

Part 1　基本問題

1 (1) linguist　(2) renowned

　　(3) wants

2 (1) what, would, like　(2) sprung up

　　(3) for which　(4) result in

3 (1) You'll be allowed to play outside

　　(2) was being isolated from the other passengers

　　(3) condemned me for telling a lie

4 (1)（例）All was going well until it suddenly started raining.

　　(2)（例）None of the students knew the

answer to the question.

(3)（例）Thanks to the internet, the song became popular overnight.

(4)（例）Children should be taught to follow the rules of society.

解説

1 (1) linguist 名「言語学者」／ linguistics 名「言語学」 (2) renowned 形「名高い」。be renowned for ～「～で名高い」／ renown 名「名声」 (3) A as well as B「B と同様 A も」では A に内容上の重点が置かれるため，動詞の人称・数は A に一致させる。ここでは Lucy（3人称単数）に合わせて wants とする。

2 (1)「音楽のない世界で暮らす」というのは現在の事実に反する状況なので，I wonder 以下の間接疑問に仮定法過去を用いる。I wonder what it would be like to do. で「～するのはどのようなものだろうか」となる。 (2) spring up「急に現れる」 (3)「それら（＝ only a few paintings）のために国際的な評価を得ている」と考えて，〈前置詞＋関係代名詞〉の for which を入れる。 (4)「…食べ過ぎると，お腹が痛くなるという結果になる」と考えて result in ～ を入れる。

3 (1) will be allowed to do「～することが認められるだろう」 (2) was being isolated は過去進行形の受動態で，「隔離されていた」という意味。 (3)〈condemn ＋ O（人）＋ for ～ ing〉「～したとして人を責める［非難する］」

4 (1) go well「（物事が）うまくいく，順調に進む」 (2) none of ～ は「（3つ以上）のうちどれも…ない，（3人以上）のうちだれも…ない」という全否定を表す。 (3) become popular overnight「一夜にして人気になる」 (4)「～するように教えられるべきである」は should be taught to do で表す。

Part 2 基本問題

1 (1) mimicking (2) teeth
(3) lungs

2 (1) vowel, consonant
(2) distinctions between
(3) head start (4) at birth
(5) important factor

3 (1) Remember to tighten the lid on the jar
(2) have a lot in common to talk about
(3) What if all the rain forests disappeared

4 (1)（例）The team is involved in restoring historical buildings.
(2)（例）The noise was so loud that he plugged his ears with his fingers.
(3)（例）I'm not sure where to place the vase.
(4)（例）By the time I came home from shopping, it had already become dark outside.

解説

1 (1) mimic 動「～をまねする，模倣する」は規則動詞だが，過去形は mimicked，～ ing 形は mimicking となる。 (2) tooth 名「歯」の複数形 teeth を選ぶ。 (3) lung 名「肺」は左右に2つあるので，複数形 lungs で用いる。

2 (1) vowel 名「母音」，consonant 名「子音」 (2) distinction 名「特徴，差異」のあとに続く前置詞は between。動詞形は distinguish「区別する」。 (3) have a head start「（ほかよりも）先にスタートを切る」 (4) at birth「生まれたときには」 (5) factor 名「要因，要素」

3 (1) remember to do「忘れずに～する」を命令文で使う。tighten the lid on ～「～のふたを締める」 (2) have O in common「O を共通に持つ，O を共有する」。この文では a lot to talk about「話すべき多くのこと」が O だが，to talk about は in common のあとに置かれている。 (3)〈What if ＋仮定法過去？〉で「もし～したらどうなるだろうか」という慣用表

現。文全体の意味は「すべての熱帯雨林が地球上から消滅したら，どうなるだろうか」となる。

4 (1) be involved in 〜ing「(活動・事業など)に関わっている，関与している」 (2) plug *one's* ears with 〜「耳に〜で栓をする」 (3)「どこに〜したらよいか」は where to *do* で表す。 (4) by the time「〜するときまでに(は)」は，これ全体が接続詞の働きをする。

Part 3　基本問題

1 (1) assuredly　　(2) continuously
(3) initial　　(4) throat

2 (1) Get close to　　(2) highly limited
(3) about trying　　(4) vibrate

3 (1) the very best movie I have ever watched
(2) You will not be able to distinguish
(3) understand what is being said by reading lips

4 (1)(例) The powerful hurricane is approaching the state of Florida.
(2)(例) The more you practice, the better you'll become at playing the piano.
(3)(例) The teacher corrected some grammatical errors in my English letter.
(4)(例) The book will tell you about what happened to the Titanic.

解説

1 (1) assuredly 副「確かに」／assured 形「確かな，確信して」 (2) continuously 副「断続的に」／continuous 形「断続的な」 (3) take the initial step toward 〜「〜に向けて第一歩を踏み出す」 (4) go down *one's* throat「(食べ物が)のどを通る」／go down *one's* cheeks「(涙が)ほおを伝って流れ落ちる」

2 (1) get close to 〜「〜に近寄る」 (2) highly

limited「非常に限られている」 (3) What about 〜 ing?「〜してはどうですか」と提案する表現。How about 〜 ing? のほうが口語的。 (4) vibrate 動「振動する」。〈feel＋O＋動詞の原形〉「O が〜するのを感じる」の知覚動詞構文に注意。

3 (1) the very best 〜 で「まさしく最高の〜」。very は最上級を強調する。全文の意味は「これは私が今までに見た中でまさに最高の映画です」となる。 (2)〈will be able to *do*〉「〜できるだろう」。distinguish between 〜「(2つのもの・人の違い)を区別する」 (3) what is being said「話されていること」。〈be being ＋過去分詞〉は現在進行形の受動態。read lips「唇の動きから発話内容を読み取る，読唇する」

4 (1) approach 動「〜に接近する」は他動詞なので，前置詞は不要。 (2)「〜すればするほど…」を〈The＋比較級＋S＋V, the＋比較級＋S＋V〉で表す。文前半では「練習する量」が問題なので，The harder you practice ではなく，The more you practice とする。 (3) correct some grammatical errors「文法上の誤りをいくつか直す」 (4)「〜に起きたこと」は，関係代名詞 what を使って，what happened to 〜で表す。

Part 4　基本問題

1 (1) mathematics　　(2) take away
(3) interpret

2 (1) become available
(2) better off　　(3) In, heyday
(4) When it comes　 (5) literacy

3 (1) tends to exaggerate what happened to him
(2) be better off studying for the test
(3) The average skill level of the team is

4 (1)(例) The disease prevails mainly in tropical regions.

(2) (例) It's no surprise that he won the championship in the tournament.

(3) (例) You can choose either cake or ice cream for dessert.

(4) (例) On the way to shopping, I saw a rainbow in the sky.

解説

1 (1) mathematics 名「数学」／ mathematic 形「数学の」 (2) take away「～を片付ける」／ take over「～を引き継ぐ」 (3) interpret 動「～を通訳する，解釈する」／ interpreter 名「通訳者」

2 (1) become available「入手［利用］可能になる」 (2) better off は well off「暮らし向きがよい」の比較級表現。 (3) in the heyday of ～「～の全盛期に」 (4) when it comes to ～「～の話になると，～に関しては」 (5) literacy 名「読み書きの能力」。cf. literacy rate「識字率」

3 (1) tend to do「～する傾向がある」。exaggerate 動「～を大げさに言う，誇張する」 (2) will be better off ～ing「～したほうがよい」 (3) the average ～「平均的な～」

4 (1) prevail in ～「（病気などが）～で広がる，蔓延する」 (2) It's no surprise that …「…は当然である，…も不思議はない」 (3) choose either A or B「A または B のどちらかを選ぶ」 (4) on the way to ～「～へ行く途中で」。on one's way to ～とも言う。cf. on the way from ～「～から戻る途中で」

発展問題

(1) 耳の不自由な人がテレビ番組の内容を理解するのを助ける

(2) 耳の不自由な人がテレビ番組の音声部分を楽しめるように，初めてテレビ・キャプションが使用されたこと。

(3) turn off the text displayed on the screen

(4) watch the captions

(5) イ

(6) ア，オ

解説

(1) The main purpose of captions is to … で始まる第1段落第3文で，テレビ放送におけるキャプションの目的を説明している。

(2) 第3段落第2文を参照。〈so that S can V〉の構文の that 以下で，料理番組にキャプションが導入された〈目的〉を述べている。

(3) 第4段落第2文を参照。did not give viewers the option to … on the screen「視聴者に画面に表示される文字を消すという選択肢を与えていなかった」とあるので，この to のあとに続く8語を抜き出して答える。

(4) 下線部④を含む whether they needed to or not は，「彼ら（＝viewers 視聴者）がそうする必要があるかないかにかかわらず」という意味。直前に出てきた watch the captions が省略されていると考える。

(5) 〈enable＋O＋to do〉「O が～することを可能にする」の不定詞構文となるように，イの enabling を選ぶ。この enabling 以下は，〈付帯状況〉を表す分詞構文で，「キャプション表示オプション」によって耳の不自由な人ができるようになることを補足的に説明している。

(5) ア 選択肢の訳 「言葉以外の要素がしばしばテレビのキャプションに記述されるのは，画面上で何が起きているかを理解するために不可欠だからである」 第2段落第2文の内容と一致。これが正解の1つ目。 イ 選択肢の訳 「初期のキャプション・システムでは，人々がそれを使用したいときにオプション機器を購入する必要があった」 第2段落第3文の最後に without relying on additional devices「別途に機器を追加することなく」とある内容とくいちがう。 ウ 選択肢の訳 「『フレンチ・シェフ』は，クローズド・キャプション・システムを導入したあ

と，アメリカ国内のテレビ視聴者の間で人気が出た」 第3段落では，『フレンチ・シェフ』の番組自体の人気については何も述べていない。 エ 選択肢の訳 「クローズド・キャプション・システムの発明は，テレビのバリアフリー化を実現するための転機となった」 第3段落第3～4文の主旨と不一致。転機となったのは，1972年にオープン・キャプション方式が初めて料理番組に導入されたことであった。 オ 選択肢の訳 「1980年になってようやくクローズド・キャプションの技術がテレビ番組で実用化された」 第4段落第3文の内容と一致。〈It was not until ～ that ...〉は「～になって初めて…した」という意味の強調構文。

〈全訳〉
TV キャプション
　今日，日本国内で制作されるテレビ番組のほとんどは，①キャプション(字幕 ― 現在表示されている内容を説明する文章または単語のグループ)付きで放送されている。視聴者は放送中に「字幕表示」モードに切り替えることにより，この文字情報を利用することができる。キャプションの主な目的は，耳の不自由な人がテレビ番組の内容を理解するのを助けるためである。
　キャプションは基本的に，番組の音声部分をその都度文字に起こすものであり，言葉以外の要素についての説明も含まれることが多い。特にドラマでは，効果音，音楽，話し方，話者の特定など，音声以外の要素が画面上の出来事を理解するために極めて重要となる。このようなキャプションを読むことにより，耳の不自由な人は，別途に機器を追加することなく，テレビ番組のコンテンツを楽しんだり，情報を利用したりすることができる。
　TV キャプションの歴史は，1972年8月5日，WGBH の料理番組『フレンチ・シェフ』(The French Chef)で，アメリカ人シェフのジュリア・チャイルドが視聴者にチキンのレシピを教えたときから始まった。この料理番組では，耳の不自由なアメリカ人がこの全国放送のテレビ番組の音声部分を楽しめるように，テレビ・キャプションが使用された。②これはまさに画期的な試みであり，耳の不自由な人に対してテレビの世界への道を開いたのである。実際，『フレンチ・シェフ』以降，キャプション付きの番組はテ

レビ体験の新たな標準となった。
　③初期のキャプション付きテレビ番組の重大な問題の1つは，④視聴者がそれを必要とするか否かにかかわらず，テレビ画面上に表示されるキャプションを常時見ていなければならないということであった。この方法はオープン・キャプションと呼ばれ，視聴者が画面に表示される文字を消すという選択肢が与えられていなかった。この問題は，1980年にアメリカの一部のテレビ番組でクローズド・キャプションが実用化されるまで続いた。
　それ以来，キャプション技術は飛躍的に向上した。キャプションはより正確で精密になり，どのテレビでも広く利用できる。現在では，テレビ放送だけでなく，インターネット上のストリーミング・サービスでもキャプション表示のオプションが提供されており，耳が不自由な人が必要な情報にアクセスできることを⑤可能にしている。キャプションは，バリアフリー社会を推進する上で必要不可欠なものとなったのである。

Lesson 7　　　　　　　　　(pp.40-45)
How Weight Training Changes the Brain in Rats

Part 1　基本問題

1 (1) resistance　　(2) cellular
　　(3) dementia　　(4) plasticity

2 (1) prop up　　(2) in turn
　　(3) To, chagrin　　(4) implications

3 (1) It is impossible for us to reverse
　　(2) Reducing the amount of plastic waste is important
　　(3) The name of the actor just eludes me

4 (1)(例) The library has a wealth of interesting books for us to read.
　　(2)(例) The firefighter used a ladder to rescue the cat in the tree.
　　(3)(例) Left unchecked, the population of rats will increase rapidly.
　　(4)(例) Eating healthy food helps you gain strength.

解説
1 (1) resistance 名「抵抗(力)」／ resistant 形「抵抗力のある」　(2) cellular 形「細胞の」

25

／ cellar 名「地下貯蔵室」 (3) dementia 名「認知症」／ inflammation 名「炎症」 (4) plasticity 名「可塑性」／ plasticize 動「～を可塑化する」

2(1) prop up the economy「景気のてこ入れを行う」 (2) in turn「今度は」 (3) To one's chagrin「残念なことに，口惜しいことに」 (4) have considerable implications for ～「～に相当の影響が及ぶ」

3(1) reverse 動「～を反転させる,逆転させる」 (2) reduce the amount of plastic waste「プラスチックごみの量を減らす」 (3) elude 動「(人の記憶)から逃げる」。しばしば「思い出せないもの」(人の名前など)を主語に，人を目的語にして用いる。

4(1) a wealth of ～「たくさんの～，大量の～」 (2) ladder 名「はしご」 (3)「放置されれば」を過去分詞の分詞構文 Left unchecked で表す。leave ～ unchecked は「(好ましくない状態)を抑制せずにそのままにしておく」という意味。population は「人口」のほか「(生物の)個体数」の意味でも用いる。 (4) gain strength「体力がつく」

Part 2　基本問題

1(1) molecular　　(2) collaborators
(3) linkage　　　(4) impairment
(5) rewards

2(1) muscles　　(2) order to
(3) reached, top　　(4) linked to
(5) testing, effects

3(1) injected the patient's arm with a vaccine
(2) are related to each other
(3) induced everyone to come

4(1)(例)It is not yet clear when the tunnel will be reopened.
(2)(例)The plant species is known to exist only in tropical regions.

(3)(例)Far less has been known about how space was created.

解説

1(1) molecular 形「分子の」／ cognitive 形「認知に関する」 (2) collaborator 名「共同作業者」／ collaboration 名「協力, 共同制作」 (3) linkage 名「連関, 連動」／ relation 名「関係」 (4) impairment 名「機能障害」／ impair 動「～を損なう」 (5) reward 名「報酬, 報い」／ award 名「賞, 賞金」

2(1) muscle 名「筋肉」。綴りと発音に注意。 (2) in order to do「～するために」(目的) (3) reach the top of ～「～の頂上[てっぺん]にたどり着く」 (4) link ～ to …「～を…と結び付ける[関連づける]」の受け身形。 (5) test the effects of ～「～の効果を検証する」

3(1) inject ～ with …「～に…を注入する」 (2) be related to each other「互いに関連し合っている」 (3)〈induce＋O＋to do〉「O が～するように仕向ける」

4(1)「いつ S が V するかはまだはっきりしない」を It is not yet clear when S＋V で表す。 (2) be known to do「～することで知られている」 (3)「はるかに少ないこと」＝far less を主語にして，動詞部には現在完了形の受動態 has been known を用いる。

Part 3　基本問題

1(1) microscopically　(2) untouched
(3) outcome　　　(4) progressively

2(1) got loose　　(2) individually wrapped
(3) accuracy　　(4) Meanwhile
(5) whereas

3(1) catch up to the level of math
(2) are similar to those of the flu
(3) might have left your umbrella on the bus

4(1)(例)Our opinions differ because we see

things from different points of view.

(2)(例)The dam construction work is lagging far behind schedule.

(3)(例)By the time we arrived, the museum had already closed.

(4)(例)The sky darkened as the sun went down.

解説

1(1) microscopically 副「顕微鏡を使って」／ microscopic 形「顕微鏡を用いた」 (2) untouched 形「触れられていない，手つかずの」／ unchecked 形「抑制されない」 (3) output 名「生産高，産出高」／ outcome 名「結果，結末」。come out「～という結果になる」から派生した名詞。 (4) progressively 副「徐々に」／ willingly 副「積極的に」

2(1) get loose「(ひもなどが)ほどける」。loose「ゆるい，ほどけた」⇔ tight「きつい」 (2) individually 副「個々に，一つ一つ[一人一人]別々に」＜ individual 形「個々の，個人の」，名「個人」 (3) with accuracy「正確に」 (4) meanwhile 副「その間に」 (5) whereas 接「その一方で」

3(1) catch up to ～「(水準など)に追いつく」。catch up with ～とほぼ同意。 (2) those は〈the＋直前に出てきた複数名詞〉の繰り返しを避けるために用いられており，ここでは the symptoms の代用。 (3)〈助動詞 might ＋have＋過去分詞〉「～したのかもしれない」は，過去の行為・出来事に関する話者の現在の推量を表す。

4(1) differ 動「異なる」。from different points of view「異なった視点から」 (2) lag behind ～「～より遅れている」。far「はるかに」は〈強調〉の副詞。 (3) by the time「～するときまでに」は，これ全体で接続詞と同じ働きをする。「美術館に着いたとき」(過去の時点)を基準にして，それまでに完了していた出来

事を過去完了形で表す。 (4) darken 動「暗くなる」＜ dark 形「暗い」

Part 4 基本問題

1(1) rarely　(2) Enzymes　(3) remodel　(4) inflame

2(1) look into　(2) full of　(3) kick-start　(4) resembles, appearance　(5) in effect

3(1) is suggestive of a gas leak

(2) you strap your seatbelt on

4(1)(例)The weather forecast tells you whether it will rain tomorrow.

(2)(例)The equipment will be helpful for those with physical impairments.

(3)(例)Who doesn't like to eat ice cream on a hot summer day?

(4)(例)Most buses have their engines in the rear.

解説

1(1) rarely 副「めったに」は，頻度が非常に少ないことを表す準否定の副詞。一方，barely 副は「かろうじて～する」(肯定)と「ほとんど～ない」(準否定)の2つの意味で用いられるが，ここでは不適。 (2) enzyme 名「酵素」／ neuron 名「ニューロン，神経細胞」 (3) remake 動「～を作り直す」／ remodel 動「～を改造する，リフォームする」 (4) inflame 動「～に炎症を起こさせる」／ inflammation 名「炎症」

2(1) look into ～ ing「～することを検討する」 (2) be full of ～「(容器などが)～でいっぱいである」。類義表現の be *filled* with ～「～でいっぱいである」は，しばしば感情表現に用いられる。(例)Her heart *was filled with* sorrow.「彼女の心は悲しみでいっぱいだった」 (3) kick-start「～を始める，～に弾みをつける」 (4) resemble ～ in appearance「～と外見が似ている」 (5) この in effect は「事

実上, 実質的に」という意味の副詞句。なお, 形容詞句として「(法律などが)発効して」の意味でも用いる。(例) The new law will be *in effect* next spring.「その新しい法律は来春発効となる」

3 (1) be suggestive of ～「～を示唆している, ～を思わせる」 (2) strap *one's* seatbelt on「シートベルトを締める」

4 (1) 〈tell + O₁(人) + O₂(whether 節)〉「人に…かどうかを伝える」 (2) those with physical impairments「身体上の障害を抱えた人々」の those は people と同意。*cf.* those who ～「～する人々」 (3) Who doesn't ～? は修辞疑問文。形式上は否定疑問文だが, 内容的には「～が好きでない人があろうか(ありはしない)」→「だれでも好きである」という〈強い肯定〉を表す。 (4) in the rear「(乗り物などの)後部に」。*cf.* a rear seat「後部座席」, rear-view mirror「バックミラー」

発展問題

(1) 筋力の維持／病気と闘うための免疫システムの強化／体重のコントロール
(2) 適度の運動または激しい運動をすること／認知機能のスコア
(3) how well your brain is functioning
(4) 毎日短時間でも運動に時間を使う
(5) イ, オ

解説

(1) 第1段落第5文で, 運動の代表的な健康効果 (health benefits) を3つ挙げている。
(2) 第2段落第3文の内容を踏まえて答える。
(3) 下線部③のあとのダッシュではさまれた補足説明の中の間接疑問 how well your brain is functioning「脳がいかに活発に機能しているか」を抜き出す。
(4) 直前の文の動名詞句 dedicating even a short amount of time to regular exercise every

day の内容を答える。
(5) ア 選択肢の訳 「多くの人が毎日欠かさず運動をしているにもかかわらず, その健康効果に気づいている人は少ない」 第1段落第1文の内容と不一致。 イ 選択肢の訳 「研究者たちは, 適度な運動と活発な運動のどちらもより高い認知能力に関連していることを発見した」 第2段落第3文の主旨と一致。これが正解の1つ目。 ウ 選択肢の訳 「研究者たちは, 4,000人を超える参加者から長期間にわたって集めたデータを分析した」 第2段落第1文と不一致。more than 4,000 participants は正しいが, for a long period of time が誤り。実際には実験は1週間連続で行われたもので, 「長期間」ではない。 エ 選択肢の訳 「運動をする期間が長ければ長いほど, 人々は実行機能において優れたパフォーマンスを示した」 第3段落では, 運動をする期間の長さについては言及されていない。 オ 選択肢の訳 「毎日欠かさずに運動を行うことが認知機能に長期的にどのような影響を与えるかはまだ明らかではない」 第4段落第2文の主旨と一致。これが正解の2つ目。

＜全訳＞
運動は記憶力を高めるか
　健康志向の傾向が定着している今日, 毎日欠かさず体を動かすことの大切さを認識する人が増えている。1日を必ずジョギングで始める人もいる。また, 仕事帰りにジムで運動して汗を流すために多額のお金を使う人もいる。実際, 適度な運動, あるいは激しい運動には①多くの健康効果がある。そうした運動は, 筋力を維持し, 病気と闘うための免疫システムを強化し, また体重をコントロールするのに役立つ。しかし, 短時間の運動がいかに記憶力や思考力を高めるかを考えたことはあるだろうか。
　2023年1月に『疫学と公衆衛生』(*Journal of Epidemiology & Community Health*)誌に掲載された最近の研究で, 研究者たちは1日24時間, 1週間連続で活動モニターを装着したイギリスの約4,500人のデータを追跡

した。②そのデータをもとに，彼らは人々の活動レベルが短期記憶，問題解決能力，そして物事を処理する能力にどのような影響を与えるかを分析した。研究者たちは，適度の運動または激しい運動をすることは，大部分の時間を座って過ごしたり，寝て過ごしたり，穏やかな活動をしたりしている人よりも，③認知機能のスコア ― 脳がいかに活発に機能しているかを示すスコア ― が大幅に高くなる結果につながることを発見した。激しい運動とは，一般にはランニング，水泳，自転車で上り坂をこぐことなどを含む。一方，適度の運動とは，いつもより速いペースで歩くことや，心拍数を加速させるような活動のことを言う。

最も注目すべき発見のひとつは，一定期間トレーニングを行った人はワーキング・メモリー(作業記憶)に改善が見られたことである。また，彼らはエグゼクティブ・プロセス(実行機能) ― 仕事の計画，効果的な時間管理，戦略的な選択など，複雑な思考，問題解決，意思決定を必要とする高次の認知機能 ― においても，より優れたパフォーマンスを示した。

研究者によれば，10分未満の運動を行うだけでも認知レベルを高めることができるという。運動が認知の健康に及ぼす長期的な影響については，さらなる研究が必要である。しかし，体を動かすのが好きでない人でも，毎日短時間でも運動に時間を使うのはよいことかもしれない。④このような習慣を今日から始めることで，あなたは残りの人生も認知の健康を享受し続けることができるかもしれない。今日，その一歩を踏み出してみてはいかがだろうか。

Lesson 8 (pp.46-51)
How to Change People's Minds

Part 1 基本問題

1 (1) herd (2) inclination
(3) inaccurate (4) approval

2 (1) faced with (2) worked well
(3) bond with
(4) without, shadow, doubt
(5) cast out (6) came into conflict

3 (1) considered what was laid before her
(2) The meeting seemed to last
(3) has not been made clear

4 (1)(例) Masao persuaded his friends to go to the park with him.
(2)(例) We tried to persuade her, but she would not change her mind.
(3)(例) The information we got turned out to be false.

解説

1 (1) どちらも「群れ」を表す名詞だが，flock は「(鳥・ヒツジ・ヤギなどの)群れ」，herd は「(ウシ・ウマなどの)群れ」のこと。
(2) inclined 形「傾いた，〜の傾向がある」／ inclination 名「傾向」 (3) accurate 形「正確な」／ inaccurate 形「不正確な」 (4) approval 名「承認，承諾」／ approve 動「承認する，認可する」

2 (1) be faced with 〜「〜に直面している」 (2) work well together「一致協力する」 (3) bond with 〜「〜と仲良くなる」 (4) without a shadow of a doubt「露ほども疑わずに」。a shadow of 〜 は「わずかな〜」。 (5) cast out「〜を追放する」の受け身形。be cast out of 〜 で「〜から追放される」という意味。 (6) come into conflict over 〜「〜をめぐって対立する」

3 (1) what was laid before her「彼女の目の前に置かれているもの」が直訳。全文の意味は「彼女は決断を下す前に目の前の状況をじっくりと考えた」。 (2) seem to do「〜するように思われる」は話者の主観を表す。 (3) 〈make＋O＋C(形容詞)〉の受け身形の現在完了形。

4 (1) 〈persuade＋O＋to do〉「〜するように人を説得する」。過去形で使うと，説得の結果，O が to do が表す行為を実際にしたことを意味する。 (2)「O を説得しようとした」は，tried to persuade O とする。上記(1)で述べた理由から，persuaded her, but ... は不可。 (3)「〜だとわかる」は turn out to be 〜 で表す。false「誤った」⇔ true「本当の」

Part 2　基本問題

1 (1) allies　(2) disciples
(3) pragmatic　(4) protector

2 (1) belief　(2) rather than
(3) care how　(4) For lack
(5) most likely

3 (1) cares a lot about her friends
(2) revealed a better way to handle the issue
(3) When having to choose between the two

4 (1)(例) The red scarf will make you look more charming[attractive].
(2)(例) My grandmother was happy to adopt the cat.
(3)(例) Reading English books can be helpful to improve your vocabulary.

解説

1 (1) ally 名「同盟」。ここでは主語が The two countries で，空所前に an がないので，複数形 allies とする。　(2) disciple 名「弟子，信奉者」／ discipline 名「規律，訓練」　(3) pragmatic 形「実用主義の，実際的な」／ pragmatism 名「プラグマティズム，実用主義」　(4) protector 名「保護者」／ protect 動「～を保護する」

2 (1) belief 名「信念」＜ believe 動「信じる」　(2) prefer A rather than B「B よりむしろ A を好む」。prefer A to B よりやや堅い言い方。(3) does not much care how ～「いかに～するかはあまり気にしない」。動詞の care は，「～を気にする」の意味では否定文・疑問文で用いるのがふつう。　(4) for lack of ～「～がないので」　(5) be likely to do「～する可能性がある」。be most likely to do は「～する可能性が非常に高い」となる。

3 (1) care a lot about ～「～のことをとても気にかける」　(2) reveal a better way to do「～するためのよりよい方法を明らかにする」

(3) When they(＝many people) are having to choose between the two から〈主節と同じ主語＋be 動詞〉が省略された形。

4 (1) 無生物主語構文。「その赤いスカーフはあなたを～に見せるでしょう」と考えて，〈S＋make＋O＋動詞の原形〉「S は O に～させる」の「動詞の原形」の部分に〈look＋形容詞〉を使う。　(2)「喜んで～する」は be happy to do で，「(動物など)を引き取る」は adopt で表す。　(3) be helpful to do「～するのに役立つ」

Part 3　基本問題

1 (1) loneliness　(2) distinctive
(3) incomparable　(4) worldviews

2 (1) convinced, to　(2) run, risk
(3) belief that　(4) torn apart
(5) clinging to

3 (1) dislike being integrated into society
(2) People living in close proximity to the park
(3) made me suspicious about the reliability

4 (1)(例) She deserves praise for her excellent work.
(2)(例) It may seem[sound] odd not to have a smartphone these days.
(3)(例) The two runners reached the finish line almost at the same moment [instant].
(4)(例) I disagree with you about that point.

解説

1 (1) lonely 形「孤独な」／ loneliness 名「孤独(感)」　(2) distinctive 形「独特の」／ distinguish 動「区別する」　(3) comparable 形「比較できる」／ incomparable 形「比類のない」　(4) worldview 名「世界観」。worldviewing(s) という単語は存在しない。

2 (1)〈convince＋O＋to do〉「(根拠・理由な

どを示して）～するように人を説得する」。persuade と同様，過去形で使う場合，O が to *do* が表す行為をしたことを意味する。 (2) run the risk of ～ ing「～するリスクを冒す」 (3) The belief that …「…という信念」の that は〈同格〉の用法。belief の具体的内容を that 節で説明している。 (4) tear ～ apart「～を引き裂く，引き離す」の受け身形。tear は不規則動詞で tear － tore － torn と変化する。 (5) cling to ～「～にしがみつく，固執する」。同様の意味を持つ熟語に stick to ～ や adhere to ～がある。

3(1) dislike being integrated into society で「社会に組み込まれることを嫌う」という意味。integrate ～ into …「～を…に組み込む」の受け身形が動名詞として dislike の目的語になっている。 (2) proximity 名「近いこと，近接」。in close proximity to ～「～の近隣に」 (3) suspicious about ～「～に疑いを持つ」。suspicious 形「（物事が）疑わしい，（人が）疑い深い」。動詞は suspect「～を疑う」，名詞は suspicion「疑い」。

4(1)「称賛を受けて当然である」を動詞 deserve 動「～に値する」を使って表す。 (2)「～するのは奇妙に思われるかもしれない」は，It may seem[sound] odd to *do* で表す。odd 形「奇妙な，風変わりな」 (3) at the same moment[instant]「同時に」 (4) disagree with ～「～（の意見・考え方）に反対である」⇔ agree with ～「～に賛成である」

Part 4　基本問題

1(1) visualize　　(2) consideration
　(3) in　　(4) eccentric
2(1) give, merit　　(2) occur between
　(3) one, the other　　(4) opposite ends
　(5) it comes
3(1) would be better spent on saving

(2) dismissed my idea as too difficult
4(1)（例）There is no sense in worrying about things you can't change.
　(2)（例）The dog was running wildly in the park, chasing a ball.
　(3)（例）We worked as a unit to complete our group project.
　(4)（例）Let's divide the cake into eight.

解説

1(1) visualize 動「～を視覚化する」／ visual 形「視覚の」 (2) consideration 名「考慮」／ considerate 形「思いやりのある」 (3)「～の方向へ」と言う場合，前置詞は in を用いる。*cf.* in all directions「四方八方へ」 (4) eccentric 形「奇妙な，奇抜な」／ essential 形「必須の」

2(1) merit 名「長所，（称賛に値する）価値」。give it merit は「それに価値を与える」→「その価値を高める」という意味。 (2) arguments occur between ～「～同士の間で口論が起きる」 (3) from one side to the other「一方の側からもう一方の側へ」 (4) on opposite ends of ～「～の両端[両側]に」 (5) when it comes to ～「～のことになると，～に関しては」

3(1) will be better spent on ～ ing「～することに使ったほうがいいだろう」。この文では saving 以下が現在の事実に反する仮定を表すため，文全体は仮定法過去となり，助動詞には would が用いられている。 (2) dismiss ～ as …「（意見など）を…だとして退ける」。as のあとには，名詞または形容詞を置く。

4(1) There is no sense in ～ ing「～してもむだだ」は動名詞を用いた There is 構文。「～のことをくよくよ悩む」は worry about ～で表す。 (2)「ボールを追いかけながら」を分詞構文の chasing a ball で表す。 (3)「一丸となって働く」は work as a unit で表す。

complete 動「～を完成させる」 (4) divide ～
into ...「～を…に(切り)分ける」。into のあと
には数詞の eight だけを続ける。

発展問題
(1) the more basic a word becomes[is]
(2) (例)長い間使われているうちに数多くの意
　　味や使い方を持つようになった基本単
　　語。(36字)
(3) ③ ウ　⑦ ア
(4) bad
(5) イ
(6) 誤った形[意味]で取り入れられた／和製英
　　語として定着した[使われるようになった]

解説
(1) 下線部①は「基本的な単語であればあるほ
　　ど，より多くの意味や用法を持つ傾向があ
　　る」という意味。言いかえ文は，これとほぼ
　　同じ内容を〈The＋比較級 ～，the＋比較級
　　…．〉の比較級構文で表している。The のあ
　　とに basic の比較級 the more basic を置き，
　　そのあとに〈S＋V〉を続ける。
(2) 下線部②の these challenging basic words
　　は，第1段落第1文の下線部①，および第2
　　文の内容を踏まえて答える。through their
　　evolution over time は「長い間変化を繰り返
　　すうちに」という意味。
(3) ③ 空所には，So many men, so many minds.
　　「人の数だけ，異なる考え方がある；十人十
　　色」ということわざの表す意味が入る。この
　　内容を言いかえた英文としては，ウ「人には
　　それぞれ固有の考え方や好みがある」が正
　　解。　⑦ 空所には Mind your own business.
　　「私のことに干渉しないで，余計なおせっか
　　いはやめて」という決まり文句。これに最も
　　近いのは，ア「私の個人的なことをあれこれ
　　きかないで」。
(4) 空所後の because of the stress from

working too hard から，「働き過ぎによるス
トレスのために，精神状態が非常に悪い」と
考える。bで始まる形容詞として適切なのは
bad。
(5) 空所直前の文の refers to a negative mental
condition「好ましくない精神状態を指す」，
および例文の内容から考えて，イの crazy
「気が狂った」が正解。
(6) 下線部⑥のあとの is introduced into the
Japanese language in an incorrect way … が
手がかり。和製英語の「ドンマイ」は Don't
mind. に由来するが，実際の英語では，I don't
mind.「私はかまいませんよ」や Don't mind
what he said.「彼が言ったことなんか気にす
るな」のような形ではよく使われるが，Don't
mind. という命令文ではめったに使われな
い。

＜全訳＞
'mind' の意味を探求する
　何年も英語を勉強した人なら，あることに気づいている
かもしれない。それは，①基本的な単語ほど，より多くの
意味や用法を持つ傾向があるということだ。英語の基本語
の多くは，古英語にルーツを持っており，長い間変化を繰
り返すうちに数多くの意味や用法を獲得してきた。'mind'
という単語は，②このように英語学習者にとって習得が難
しい基本単語の1つであろうか。辞書でこの単語を引いて
みれば，その意味の広さと深さに驚くことだろう。
　まず，'mind' は，一般に人の考え方，感じ方，知性の
使い方を意味し，しばしば慣用表現で用いられる。例えば，
"She has finally made up her mind to study abroad."（彼
女はようやく留学する決心がついた）のように言うことが
できる。また，だれかに対して「考えを変える」（change
their mind）ように説得することもできる。また，有名な
ことわざに "So many men, so many minds."（十人十色）
というものがある。これは，「③人はそれぞれ固有の考えや
嗜好を持っているので，考えや行動が異なるのは当然であ
る」という意味である。以上の例では，'mind' は日本語で
は「考え」または「考え方」と訳すことができる。
　'mind' のもう1つの重要な用法に話を移すが，この単
語は人の「精神状態」を指すのに使われる。例えば，I'm
losing my mind trying to finish this job on time.（私はこの

仕事を予定どおりに終わらせることに懸命で，もう気が狂いそうだ)と言えば，それは働き過ぎによるストレスのために，精神状態が非常に <u>悪い</u>④ことを示している。さらに慣用句の 'out of one's mind' は，たとえば "You must be out of your mind to swim in the sea on such a cold day."（こんな寒い日に海で泳ぐなんて，あなたはどうかしている)などの文に見られるように，好ましくない精神状態を指す。それは「<u>正気を失っている</u>⑤」(crazy) ことを意味する。以上の例で使われている名詞の 'mind' は，日本語では「心」または「気」を意味する。

　さらに，'mind' という単語は，日常的な多くの場面において動詞として用いられる。"Never mind."（気にするな，<u>心配するな</u>⑥)は，「ドンマイ」という誤った形で日本語に取り込まれ，典型的な和製英語の１つとなっている。"Mind your own business." は「<u>個人のプライベートなことをあ</u>⑦<u>れこれ詮索するのはやめなさい</u>」という意味の警告として用いられる。だれかに自分と友人の写真を撮ってくれるように頼むときは，"Would you mind taking our picture?"（私たちの写真を撮っていただけないでしょうか)と言えばよい。

　以上述べてきたことは，'mind' という単語に関連する意味や用法のほんの一部に過ぎない。辞書でこの単語を調べ，さらに興味深い用例を発見して，自分でこの単語についてさらに探求してみてはどうだろうか。

Lesson 9　(pp.52-57)
On Love,

Part 1　基本問題

1 (1) conclude　　　(2) theological
　　(3) uncrossable　　(4) philosophical
　　(5) permeate

2 (1) plays, role[part]　(2) pick up, pieces
　　(3) a thousand　　(4) Speak[((英))Talk] of
　　(5) gave, explanation

3 (1) can be unbearable without enough water
　　(2) What do you call the bird
　　(3) she is a most talented woman

4 (1)(例)John fell in love with a girl who spoke to him on the bus.
　　(2)(例)There are numerous stars in the sky on a clear night.

　(3)(例)Athletes need to endure a lot of training to become stronger.

解説

1 (1) include 動「〜を含む」/ conclude 動「〜と結論づける」　(2) theologically 副「神学的に」/ theological 形「神学上の」　(3) uncrossable 形「渡ることができない」/ unclimbable 形「登ることができない」　(4) philosopher 名「哲学者」/ philosophical 形「哲学上の」　(5) permeate 動「〜に充満する，浸透する」/ traverse 動「〜を横切る，横断する」

2 (1) play a central role[part] in 〜「〜において中心的な役割を果たす」　(2) pick up the pieces「かけらを拾い集める」→「(挫折・失敗などのあとで)事態を収拾する」　(3) a thousand 〜「千の〜」→「いくらでも多くの〜」　(4) speak of 〜「〜のことを話す」。ことわざの Speak of the devil, and he is sure to appear. は，and 以下を省略して，speak of the devil だけで用いられることも多い。　(5) give an explanation of 〜「〜のことを説明する」

3 (1) unbearable 形「耐えられない」。without enough water「十分な水がなければ」　(2)〈call＋O＋C〉「O(人・もの)をC(名前)と呼ぶ」のCを尋ねる疑問詞疑問文は What で始める。　(3) 並べ替え部分は「彼女はとても有能な女性である」という意味。a most talented woman のような〈a[an]＋形容詞の最上級＋名詞〉は絶対最上級と呼ばれ，比較の対象なしに，単に程度が高いことを表す。

4 (1)「〜と恋に落ちる」は fall in love with 〜で表す。　(2) numerous 形「数え切れないほど多くの」。on a clear night の前置詞 on にも注意。　(3)「(試練・トレーニングなど)に耐える」は endure で表す。

1(1) humankind　　　(2) therapist

　　(3) devastating　　　(4) affirm

　　(5) affection

2(1) beyond, scope　　(2) at least

　　(3) demands, met[satisfied]

　　(4) would not, irresponsible　(5) are to

3(1) At the heart of any culture is

　　(2) His desire to succeed seems to be
　　　stronger

　　(3) Nothing is more fun than playing games

4(1)(例)Eating nutritious food every day is
　　　essential to our health.

　　(2)(例)Many parents indulge their children
　　　with toys and games.

　　(3)(例)That is why I usually take a bus to
　　　travel a short distance.

解説

1(1) humankind 名「人類」は不可算名詞なの
で，複数形では使わない。　(2) therapy 名「治
療，〜療法」／ therapist 名「療法士，セラピスト」
(3) experience「経験」との結びつきから考え
て，devastating 形「(被害などが)壊滅的な，
衝撃的な」が適切。devastated「打撃を受け
た」は人を主語にして用いる。　(4) affirm 動
「〜を肯定する，認める」／ confirm 動「(事実
など)を確認する」(5) affection 名「愛情」／
isolation 名「孤立」

2(1) beyond the scope of 〜「〜の範囲を超
えて」(2) at least「少なくとも」は，動詞
または文全体を修飾して，最低限の事柄を挙
げる際にも用いられる。　(3) meet[satisfy]
demands「要求をかなえる」の受け身形。「要
求」の意味での demand はしばしば複数形
で用いられ，demands for 〜「〜を求める要
求」の形で用いられる。　(4) 主語の A person
with common sense に「もし常識のある人な
ら」という仮定が含まれた仮定法過去の文。

従って，助動詞は過去形の would not を用いる。
irresponsible 形「無責任な」⇔ responsible 形「責
任を果たしうる」　(5)〈if＋S＋be 動詞＋to *do*〉
「もし S が〜したいと思うなら」

3(1) at the heart of 〜「〜の中心に」。〈前置
詞句＋be 動詞＋S〉の倒置文で，文末の its
language が主語。　(2)〈seem to be 〜〉「〜で
あるように思われる」は〈話者の主観〉を表す。
主語の His desire to succeed は「成功したい
という彼の願望」という意味。　(3)〈Nothing is
more 〜 than ...〉「…より〜なものはない」。比
較級を用いて，最上級と同じ内容を表した文。

4(1) 動名詞 Eating nutritious food every day
を主語にする。「〜にとって欠かせない」は be
essential to 〜で表す。　(2) indulge 〜 with
…「〜を…で甘やかす」　(3)「そういうわけで
〜」は That is why 〜の形で表す。travel a
short distance「短距離を移動する」。英語の
travel は，「旅行する」だけでなく，単に「(一
定の距離を)移動する」場合にも用いる。

Part 3　基本問題

1(1) egocentric　　　(2) eradicate

　　(3) euphoria　　　(4) unrealistic

　　(5) fanciful

2(1) reckoned with　(2) belongs to

　　(3) conceive of　　(4) willing to

　　(5) mind on

3(1) emerged as a power to be reckoned with

　　(2) feel the same way toward their favorite
　　　book

　　(3) The media may give us the false sense

4(1)(例)If you use your time efficiently, you
　　　can get a lot of things done in one
　　　day.

　　(2)(例)We should promote recycling for the
　　　benefit of the environment.

　　(3)(例)The Earth and the other planets

revolve around the sun.

1(1) egocentrism 名「自己中心主義」／ egocentric 形「自己中心主義的な」 (2) eradicate 動「～を根絶する，撲滅する」／ radicate 動「(植物など)を根付かせる」 (3) euphoria 名「幸福感」／ euphoric 形「有頂天の」 (4) insincere 形「不誠実な」／ unrealistic 形「非現実的な」 (5) fancy 名「空想，想像」／ fanciful 形「想像上の，架空の」

2(1) reckon with ～「((否定文で))～を考慮に入れる」。この文では neither of ～「(2つ・2人の)どちらも～ない」が否定の意味を表す。 (2) belong to ～「～に属する，～のものである」。*cf.* personal belongings「個人の持ち物」 (3) conceive of ～「～を想像する，思い描く」 (4) be willing to *do*「喜んで[進んで]～する」 ⇔ be unwilling to *do*「しぶしぶ～する，～することを嫌がる」 (5) keep *one's* mind on ～「～に集中する」(≒concentrate on ～)

3(1) 全文は「その初出場チームは考慮されるべき存在として現れた」という意味。a power のあとに受け身形の不定詞 to be reckoned with を続けることに注意。reckon with 全体が他動詞として扱われるため，前置詞の with を切り離さないこと。 (2) feel the same way toward ～「～に対して同じように感じる」 (3) give ～ the false sense that …「～に…という錯覚を与える」

4(1)「(用事など)を済ませる」は get ～ done で表す。 (2)「環境のために」は for the benefit of the environment で表す。for the benefit of ～は「～にとって益となるように」が文字通りの意味。 (3) revolve around ～「～の周りを回る」

Part 4　基本問題

1(1) instinctual　　　　(2) satisfaction

(3) enrich　　　　(4) expend

2(1) take credit　　　　(2) in an effort

(3) goes[is] beyond　　　　(4) run, course

(5) worth hiking

3(1) under the influence of their natural instincts

(2) let me help you set the table

4(1)(例)Sarah chose to stay home and read a book instead of going out.

(2)(例)He is proud of having won (the) first prize in the speech contest.

(3)(例)Birds have an instinct to build nests to keep their eggs safe.

(4)(例)We cannot start the meeting until all the members are here.

1(1) instinct 名「本能」／ instinctual 形「本能の」。形容詞は instinctive のほうが一般的。 (2) satisfaction 名「満足」／ satisfied 形「満足した」。give ～ a sense of satisfaction で「～に満足感を与える」という意味。 (3) enrich 動「～を豊かにする」／ rich 形「豊かな」 (4) expend 動「～を費やす」／ expand 動「～を拡大する，拡張する」

2(1) take credit for ～「～の手柄を認められる」 (2) in an effort to *do*「～しようと努力して」 (3) go beyond ～「(能力・理解など)を超える」 (4) run its course「(病気などが)自然に治る，(事態などが)自然に収まる」 (5) be worth ～ ing「～するだけの価値がある」

3(1) under the influence of ～「～の影響を受けて」 (2)〈let＋O＋動詞の原形〉「Oに～させる」の構文の「動詞の原形」の部分に〈help＋O＋動詞の原形〉「Oが～するのを手伝う」を組み込む。

4(1) choose to *do*「～することを選ぶ」。「～する代わりに」は instead of ～を用いる。 (2) be proud of ～「～を誇りに思っている」。「ス

ピーチコンテストで1位になった」のは過去の出来事なので，完了形の動名詞（having＋過去分詞）で表す。　　(3)「〜する本能がある」は have an instinct to *do* で表す。「巣を作る」と言う場合，動詞には build を使う。

発展問題

(1) how precious their pets are to them
(2) specific activities we love
(3) ウ
(4) メモを取ったり記録を取ったりする行為が純粋に好きであること。(30字)
(5) 自分の好きな特定のアクティビティを積極的に追求すること。
(6) イ

解説

(1) 下線部①は，〈tell＋O₁（人）＋O₂（もの）〉の O₂の一部で，感嘆文 how precious their pets are to them がそのまま名詞節として埋め込まれた形である。

(2) 下線部②の them は直前の these activities と同様，第2段落第1文のダッシュ（―）でくくられた specific activities we love「私たちが好きな特定のアクティビティ」を指す。

(3) 下線部③の cut back on 〜は「〜を切り詰める，削減する」（≒reduce）という意味の句動詞。「費用を切り詰める」という意味になるので，ウの use less money「出費を抑える」が正解。

(4) 第3段落第6文後半の the fact is that のあとに続く内容を踏まえて答える。genuinely 副「純粋に」。the act of 〜 ing「〜という行為」の of は〈同格〉を表し，of 以下の動名詞が act の具体的内容を説明している。

(5) 下線部⑥の doing so は，直前の pursuing them positively を指すが，代名詞の them は if 節内の specific activities，つまり「あなたが好きな特定のアクティビティ」を指す。こ

の内容を必ず答えに含める。

(6) 文頭の moreover「さらに，そのうえ」は，情報を加えるディスコース・マーカー（談話標識）。同じ名詞 career「キャリア」を含む第5文の直前に置くと，第5文は欠文の内容を補強することとなり，前後の文脈が通る。

＜全訳＞

好きなことを追求する

　私たちは好きなものについて語らずにはいられないものである。サッカーファンなら，自分の好きなチームや選手について，あるいはこれまでに観戦した中で最も興奮した試合について熱く語るかもしれない。ペットを飼っている人は，飼い猫や飼い犬がどのようにして家族の一員になったか，そして自分にとってペットがどれほど大切な存在であるかを話すかもしれない。

　また，写真を撮ったり，野鳥を観察したり，ガーデニングをしたりといった，いわゆる趣味 ― 私たちが好きな特定のアクティビティ ― についても話したがるものである。こうしたアクティビティに共通するのは，屋内であれ屋外であれ，それらを予算と時間の範囲内で自分なりに楽しむことができるという点である。必ずしも高価な機器やガジェットが必要なわけではないし，これらの趣味がだれでも入手可能であることに変わりはない。こうしたアクティビティに熱中する度合いが強ければ強いほど，出費を抑えるのは難しくなる。

　別の側面に話を移すと，私たちの何かに対する愛は，しばしば個人的な習慣という形をとる。例えば，日常生活のあらゆる場面でメモを取るのが大好きな人がいる。彼らはいつもペンとノートを持ち歩き，アイディアや覚えておくべきことを書き留める。デジタル時代においては，スマートフォンやパソコンの日記アプリやカレンダーアプリを使って，自分の身に起きるあらゆる事柄を記録しようとする人がいる。自分の体験をツイートする人さえいる。このような行動は個人的な習慣と見ることもできるが，事実として，こうした人々はメモを取ったり記録を取ったりする行為が純粋に好きだということである。

　もしあなたが特定のアクティビティが好きなら，それを積極的に追求することを考えるとよい。そうすることで，あなたは日常生活を豊かにする方法を数多く見つけることができる。例えば，料理を作ることが大好きなら，自分のオリジナルレシピをソーシャルメディアプラットフォームで共有すれば，充実感が得られるかもしれない。さらには，好きなアクティビティを追求することによって，自分の将来のキャリアについて考えるきっかけが得られるかもしれ

ない。多くの人々が自分の大好きなものに関連したキャリアを選んできた。しかし，もし時間を忘れるほど興味を引くものが特にないのであれば，今日からそれを探し始めてみてはいかがだろうか。

Lesson 10 　　　　　　　　　　(pp.58-63)
Is Professor Feynman Sexist?

Part 1　基本問題

1 (1) velocity　　　　　(2) subtlety
　　(3) valid　　　　　　(4) freshman

2 (1) Making, accusation
　　(2) raised, objection　(3) figure out
　　(4) incapable of　　　(5) no point

3 (1) There's a discussion about how to improve
　　(2) the police officer made her look stupid

4 (1)(例) Emma accused me of eating the last piece of cake.
　　(2)(例) The professor received a letter of protest from a feminist group.
　　(3)(例) We had to stay (at) home because of the heavy rain.
　　(4)(例) Some power plants use nuclear energy to generate electricity.
　　(5)(例) The astronomer recounted what the Earth looked like from the ISS.

解説

1 (1) velocity 图「速度」／ altitude 图「高度」　(2) subtle 形「微妙な，繊細な」／ subtlety 图「繊細さ」　(3) valid 形「有効な」／ invalid 形「無効な」。「テーマパークに入れた」のだから，正解は valid。　(4) 後ろの students を修飾するので，freshman が適切。freshman(複数形 freshmen)は，アメリカで主に「大学1年生」を指す。「2年生」は sophomore，「3年生」は junior，「4年生」は senior と呼ばれる。

2 (1) make an accusation は「告訴する，告発する」，あるいは，この文のように「非難する，言いがかりをつける」の意味で用いられる。　(2) raise an objection「反対の声を上げる，異議を唱える」　(3) figure out は「(謎など)を解く，(問題)を解決する，〜を理解する」などの意味。　(4) be incapable of 〜 ing「〜することができない」⇔ be capable of 〜 ing「〜することができる」　(5) There is no point in 〜 ing「〜しても意味がない」。It is no use crying over spilt milk. という形のほうが一般的。

3 (1) There's a discussion about 〜「〜に関しては議論が行われている」。cf. There is a lot of argument about[over] 〜「〜をめぐっては多くの議論がある」　(2)〈make＋O＋動詞の原形〉の構文。ここでは「動詞の原形」の位置に〈look＋形容詞〉を置く。stupid 形「ばかな，愚かな」

4 (1)「〜したと言って O を責める」は〈accuse＋O＋of＋〜 ing〉の形で表す。　(2)「抗議の手紙」は a letter of protest。　(3) because of 〜 は「〜のために」という理由を表し，of のあとには名詞句が続く。「家にいる」は stay home または stay at home で表す。　(4)「発電所」は power plant，「発電する」は generate electricity，「核エネルギー」は nuclear energy で表す。cf. nuclear bomb「核爆弾」, nuclear weapons「核兵器」　(5) recount 動「〜を詳しく話す」。「S がどんなふうに見えたか」は what S looks like となる。look like「〜のように見える」の目的語を尋ねる疑問文なので，疑問詞には what を用いる。

Part 2　基本問題

1 (1) excerpt　　　　　(2) unsatisfactory
　　(3) affairs　　　　　(4) response

2 (1) fistful of　　　　(2) catch up

(3) in charge of   (4) glanced at

(5) giving out

3(1) was invited to speak at the conference

(2) front of the bank were several police cars

(3) awarded her a prize for winning

4(1)(例)My family has two dogs. One is black, and the other is brown.

(2)(例)I saw protestors standing near the gate.

(3)(例)Many companies replace their computers every three years or so.

(4)(例)He had to revise his essay to make it better.

解説

1(1) except 前「～を除いて」／ excerpt 名「引用, 抜粋」 (2)「次回はもっと一生懸命勉強しようと決心した」という so 以下の内容と合うように unsatisfactory 形「不満足な」を選ぶ。反対語は satisfactory 形「満足な」。 (3) personal affairs「私事, 個人的なこと」。この意味では複数形 affairs で用いる。*cf.* world affairs「国際情勢」 (4) respond 動「反応する」／ response 名「反応」

2(1) a fistful of ～「一握りの～」。fist は「握り拳, 拳固」の意。 (2) catch up with ～「～に追いつく」 (3) in charge of ～「～を担当して, ～の責任者で」 (4) glance at ～「～をちらっと見る」。1回限りの動作を表す名詞として, take a glance at ～の形でも用いる。 (5) give out ～ to …「～を…に配る」

3(1)〈invite＋O＋to do〉「O に～するように依頼[要請]する」の受け身形。speak at ～「～で講演する」 (2) 前置詞句 in front of ～を文頭に出した倒置文で,〈前置詞句＋be 動詞＋S〉の語順。通常の語順に直せば, Several police cars were in front of the bank. となる。 (3)〈award＋O₁（人）＋O₂（賞など）＋for 業績〉の

語順。

4(1) 2つのものについて,「1つは～, もう1つは…」と言うときは, One ～, the other … で表す。 (2)「O が～しているのを見る」は知覚動詞構文の〈see＋O＋現在分詞〉で表す。protestor 名「抗議者」 (3) every ～ years or so「～年おきくらいに」 (4) revise 動「～を修正する,（本など）を改訂する」。日本語の「小論文, レポート」は essay で表すことが多い。

Part 3　基本問題

1(1) trivial   (2) chant

(3) Ph.D.   (4) without

(5) remedy

2(1) As soon as   (2) remind, of

(3) suffer from   (4) on either

(5) marched down

3(1) Her presence at the party made everyone feel happier

(2) explained to her friend that

(3) Is that what you call love

4(1)(例)Her parents encouraged Kana to pursue her passion for painting.

(2)(例)Can you think of a good idea for our project?

(3)(例)He politely declined his uncle's invitation to the party.

解説

1(1) trivia 名「ささいなこと, 雑学的な知識」／ trivial 形「ささいな, つまらない」 (2) chat 動「おしゃべりする, チャットする」／ chant 動「～を一斉に唱える, 連呼する」 (3) Ph.D.「博士号」はラテン語の *Philosophiae Doctor*(((英))Doctor of Philosophy）の略。 (4) without prejudice「偏見を持たずに」 (5) remedy 名「治療法」／ solidarity 名「団結, 連帯」

2(1) as soon as ～「～するとすぐに, ～する やいなや」が導く副詞節の中では, 未来の事柄も現在形で表す。 (2) remind *A* of *B*「A（人）にB（もの・事柄）を思い出させる」 (3) suffer from ～「(病気)を患う, (困難など)に苦しむ」 (4)「～の両側に」は on either side of ～または on both sides of ～で表す。ここでは side が単数形なので, on both は不可。 (5) march down to ～「～まで行進しながら進む」

3(1) presence 名「いること, 存在」を主語とする〈make＋O＋動詞の原形〉「O に～させる」の構文。 (2) explain は目的語を2つとらない動詞なので,「人に…と説明する」は〈explain to＋人＋that 節〉の形で表す。 (3) 文全体の意味は「それがあなたが愛と呼ぶものなのですか」。関係代名詞の what は call の目的語の働きをしている。

4(1)〈encourage＋O＋to *do*〉「O に～するよう励ます」。「～に対する情熱」は passion for ～で表す。 (2)「何かよいアイディアを思いつくことができますか」と考えて, Can you think of ～? の形を用いる。 (3)「(招待・誘い)を断る」は decline で表す。

Part 4　基本問題

1(1) confess　　(2) dramatic
(3) proton　　(4) transcript

2(1) put, down　　(2) anywhere near
(3) much more　　(4) the way
(5) concerned about

3(1) different from what I actually said
(2) Don't forget to call your grandmother

4(1)(例)We looked at each other[one another] when we heard the news.
(2)(例)I remember speaking at the conference several years ago.
(3)(例)He told me that he had never been defeated in debate.
(4)(例)I have nothing to say about the matter.
(5)(例)I would like to talk about a book I have read recently.

解説

1(1) confess 動「～を告白する, 白状する」／convince 動「～を納得させる, 説得する」 (2) dramatic 形「劇的な」／drastic 形「思い切った, 抜本的な」 (3) protein 名「タンパク質」／proton 名「陽子, プロトン」 (4) transcript 名「文字に起こしたもの, 記録, 写し」／transform 動「変形する」, 名「変換」

2(1) put down「～を下ろす」 (2) anywhere near as ～ as …「((通例否定文で))とても…ほどには～でない」 (3)〈much＋比較級＋than S had imagined〉「Sが想像していたよりもはるかに～」 (4)〈the way＋S＋V〉「SがV するように」 (5) be concerned about ～「～に不安を抱いている, ～を心配している, ～に関心を持っている」

3(1) be different from ～「～と違う, 異なる」。この文では from のあとに関係代名詞節の what I actually said「私が実際に言ったこと」を続ける。 (2) Don't forget to *do*「～するのを忘れないようにしなさい」

4(1) each other および one another はどちらも代名詞なので, 自動詞のあとに使う場合は, look at のように前置詞が必要となる。なお, 主語が複数(we や they など)で人数がはっきりわからない場合, 現在では each other を用いるのが一般的である。 (2)「～したことを覚えている」は remember ～ ing で表す。「(場所)で講演する」は speak at ～。 (3) 過去のある時点までの〈経験〉を述べているので, that 節の中の動詞を過去完了形の受け身形にする。 (4) have nothing to say about ～「～に関しては何も言うことがない」 (5)「～

したいと思います」は would like to *do* で表す。

発展問題

(1) ladies and gentlemen

(2) 機内アナウンス／一方の性に特定した言葉

(3) すべての人々が例外なしに受け入れられる世界を築き上げること。（30字）

(4) What is considered gender-neutral language can change

(5) ア gender-specific　イ gender-neutral
　　ウ police officer　エ chair　オ server

(6) イ

解説

(1) 下線部①を含む a mix of both は「（その）両方の混ざったもの」という意味で，both は直前に出てきた2つのものを指す代名詞。ここでは，同じ文の中に現れる ladies および gentlemen の2つを指す。

(2) 第2段落第3文から，エア・カナダが機内アナウンスに ladies and gentlemen という呼びかけを使うのをやめたのは，「一方の性に特定した言葉を排除しようとする彼らの努力を反映した」結果だとわかる。

(3) 第3段落最終文によれば，多くの企業や団体が「一方の性に特定した考え方をできるだけ排除しようと努めている」目的とは，「すべての人々が例外なしに受け入れられる世界を築き上げる」ことだとわかる。

(4) 〈consider＋O＋C（名詞）〉の受け身は，〈元のO＋be 動詞＋considered＋C（名詞）〉の形。「何が〜とみなされるのか」を尋ねる間接疑問では，「元のO」の位置に疑問詞の what を置く。

(5) 第4段落第2文で，「一方の性に特定した」（gender-specific）語が「男女の区別のない」（gender-neutral）語に置き換えられた具体例を挙げている。この内容をもとに表を完成

させる。

(6) ア　選択肢の訳　「これまでのところ，男女の区別のない言葉を使おうという動きは航空業界でのみ見られる」　第3段落第1〜2文の内容と不一致。　イ　選択肢の訳　「最近では，'brothers and sisters' を含む男女の区別のない言葉として 'siblings'（きょうだい）が使われる」　第4段落第3文の内容と一致。ウ　選択肢の訳　「どのような言語であれ，あらゆる性差に関する偏見や固定観念を完全に排除することは不可能である」　本文の内容から外れる。

＜全訳＞

「紳士淑女の皆様」

「紳士淑女の皆様」というフレーズで始まるアナウンスを聞いたことがあるかもしれない。歴史的に，この表現はそこにいる全員が淑女か，全員が紳士か，あるいは①その両方かに関係なく，集団または聴衆に向かって話しかけるときに広く使われてきた。興味深いことに，この表現は，それが紳士であろうと淑女であろうと，話しかける相手が1人だけの場合にも使うことができる。人々は長い間これを理解し，受け入れてきた。しかし，世の中の状況は変化しつつあり，私たちの言葉の使い方は，性差に関する偏見や固定観念を取り除き，性差に基づく差別を防ぐことによって男女の性別による区別をしない方向へと変わってきている。

2019年10月，カナダの大手航空会社の1つであるエア・カナダは，②今後は客室乗務員が乗客に 'ladies and gentlemen'（紳士淑女の皆様）と挨拶することをやめると発表した。その代わりに，客室乗務員は "Good morning, everybody."（おはようございます，皆様）といった男女の区別のない挨拶を使い始めた。エア・カナダは，こうした機内アナウンスに関する方針の変更は，一方の性に特定した言葉を排除しようとする彼らの努力を反映したものだと述べた。こうした言葉の使い方の変更は，空港の搭乗ゲートで働く係員にも適用された。ドイツのルフトハンザや日本の JAL など，ほかの多くの航空会社も機内アナウンスに関する方針に同様の変更を行っている。

こうした変化は航空業界だけにとどまらない。③現在では，ますます多くの企業や団体が一方の性に特定した考え方をできるだけ排除しようとしている。このような動きは，しばしば「男女の性別による区別をしないことの促進」と

呼ばれ，男女の区別のない言葉を使うことは，すべての人々が例外なしに受け入れられる世界を築き上げるための重要な一歩だと考えられている。

英語学習者の立場からすると，一方の性に特定した言葉を男女の区別のない言葉に置き換えることには戸惑いを覚えるかもしれない。例えば，'policeman' の代わりに 'police officer' を使う，'chairman' または 'chairwoman' の代わりに 'chair' や 'chairperson' を使う，'waiter' や 'waitress' の代わりに 'server' を使う，といった具合である。最近では，'brothers and sisters' のような言葉でさえ，'siblings'（きょうだい）に置き換えられることが多い。実際，英語を母語とする人たちでさえ，男女の区別のない言葉を使うときに苦労したり，混乱したりすることがあるのだ。④どのような言葉が男女の区別のない言葉とみなされるのかは，時代とともに変化していく可能性がある。重要な点として覚えておきたいのは，私たちが毎日使っている言葉は，私たちが人をどのように理解し，どのように扱うかと密接に結びついているということである。

Lesson 11 (pp.64-69)
Language Awareness

Part 1　基本問題

1(1) revitalize　(2) steadily
(3) dialects

2(1) civil rights movement
(2) led, campaigns　(3) bear fruit
(4) on, rise　(5) no more
(6) social minorities

3(1) English was made an official language
(2) As many as 5,000 people took part in

4(1)(例)Single-use plastic bags are banned in some countries.
(2)(例)No plant would survive without water.
(3)(例)Alaska became part of the U.S. in 1867.
(4)(例)It will be almost impossible to bring back old traditions once they are lost.

解説

1(1) revitalize 動「～を活性化する」／ refurbish 名「～を改造する」　(2) steadily 副「着実に，着々と」／ steady 形「着実な」　(3) dialect 名「方言」／ tribe 名「部族」

2(1) the civil rights movement「公民権運動」。civil right は複数形となる。　(2) lead to ～「（結果として）～につながる」。lead は不規則動詞で，lead － led － led と変化する。「（社会的・政治的）運動」は campaign で表す。(3) bear fruit「（植物が）実を結ぶ」は，文字通りの意味のほか，比喩的に「（活動・計画などの）よい結果が出る」という意味でも用いられる。　(4) on the rise「（価格などが）上昇中で」　(5) no more than ～「～しか，たった～」　(6) social minorities「社会的少数者」

3(1)〈make＋O＋C（名詞）〉「O を C にする」の受け身形は〈元の O＋is＋made＋C（名詞）〉となる。official language「公用語」　(2) as many as ～「～もの多くの」は〈数の多さ〉を強調する表現。〈量の多さ〉を強調する場合は，as much as ～を用いる。

4(1) ban「～を禁止する」を受け身で用いる。「使い捨ての」は single-use「一度しか使わない」で表すことが多い。　(2)「水がなければ」＝without water に現在の事実に反する仮定が含まれるため，動詞部分に仮定法過去 would survive を用いる。　(3)「～の一部になる」は become part of ～で表す。part の前に a は付けないのがふつう。　(4) 接続詞 once「いったん～すれば」が導く節の中では，未来の事柄を表すときも動詞は現在形を用いる。bring back「～を回復させる」

Part 2　基本問題

1(1) charter　(2) oppose
(3) ratify　(4) elimination
(5) unity

2 (1) Constitution state　(2) city council

(3) proposed, revitalize

(4) went as far　(5) In addition to

3 (1) There is a strong connection between

(2) may be unwilling to speak

(3) It is no wonder that the shop attracts

4 (1)(例) In the meantime, departure time was approaching.

(2)(例) The emergence of new technology has changed the way we communicate.

(3)(例) Heavy rain considerably disrupted public transportation in the Kanto district.

解説

1 (1) chapter 名「(本などの)章」／ charter 名「憲章, 設立趣意書」　(2) oppose 動「～に反対する」／ opposition 名「反対」　(3) ratify 動「(条約を)批准する, (法律などを)承認する」／ compromise 動「～を危うくする」　(4) eliminate 動「～を取り除く, 撲滅する」／ elimination 名「除去, 撲滅」　(5) unity 名「結束, 統一」／ unite 動「一致団結する」

2 (1) 各国の「憲法」は the Constitution で表す。「憲法」の各条項は Article 9 のように表す。state 動「～を宣言する」　(2) the city council「市議会」。cf. the student council「(学校の)生徒会」　(3) propose a plan「計画を提案する」。revitalize 動「～に新たな活力を与える, ～を活性化する」。cf. vital「生命(維持)にかかわる, 極めて重要な」, vitality「活気, 活力」　(4) go as far as ～ ing「～するところまで行く」　(5) in addition to ～「～に加えて, ～のほかに」

3 (1) There is a strong connection between *A* and *B*.「A と B の間には密接な関係がある」　(2) be unwilling to *do*「～するのを嫌がる, しぶしぶ～する」⇔ be willing to *do*「喜んで～する」　(3) It is no wonder (that) ...「…は不

思議ではない, 無理もない」。It is および that はしばしば省略され, No wonder ... となる。

4 (1)「そうこうするうちに」を In the meantime で表す。「(時間が)迫っている」は自動詞 approach を進行形で使う。　(2) emergence 名「出現」< emerge 動「現れる」。〈the way＋S＋V〉「S が V する方法」は, これ全体で名詞節となり, 動詞の目的語などになる。　(3) disrupt 動「～を乱す, 混乱させる」。「公共交通機関」は public transportation。

Part 3　基本問題

1 (1) obstacle　(2) imposition

(3) unequivocally　(4) Inspectorate

(5) sovereign

2 (1) plays, role　(2) reluctant to

(3) nothing but　(4) Take

(5) proceeded to

3 (1) impose their ideas on their children

(2) regard their pets as part of

(3) want even a hint of influence from others

4 (1)(例) India became independent in 1947.

(2)(例) Every year, many tourists visit the hot spring from inside and outside Japan.

(3)(例) As far as the eye could see, there were no clouds in the sky.

解説

1 (1) obstruct 動「～を妨害する, (道などを)遮る」／ obstacle 名「障害物, 妨害物」　(2) imposition 名「(義務・負担などの)押しつけ, (税金などを)課すこと」／ position 名「地位, 位置」　(3) unequivocally 副「明白に」。unequivocal 形「明白な」。cf. equivocal 形「何通りにも解釈できる, 曖昧な」　(4) エストニアの「言語監督庁」は Language Inspectorate。inspector は「調査官, 警視正」

の意。 (5) sovereign 形「君主である，元首である」／ sovereignty 名「主権，統治権」

2 (1) play an important role in ～「～において重要な役割を果たす」 (2) be reluctant to *do*「～したがらない」 (3) nothing but ～「～だけ，ただの～」(≒only) (4) Take, for example, ～「例えば～を例にとりましょう」 (5) proceed to *do*「続けて～する」

3 (1) impose ～ on …「～を…に押しつける」 (2) regard *A* as *B*「A を B とみなす，考える」 (3) even a hint of influence from ～「～のわずかな影響さえも」。a hint of ～ は「わずかな～，～の気配」の意。

4 (1)「(国として)独立する」ことを表す 1 語の動詞は存在せず，become independent を使うのがふつう。independent 形「独立した」，independence 名「独立」 (2)「日本国内外から」は from inside and outside Japan で表せる。 (3)「雲一つなかった」は，全否定の there were no clouds で表せる。また，「見渡す限り」を表す英語表現としては，as far as the eye could see が最も一般的。ただし，× as far as my eye(s) could see とは言えない。

発展問題

(1) 戦場で重要な情報を安全に送るための解読不可能な暗号を作る(28字)
(2) 家庭内においても母語ではなく英語を使う
(3) ア
(4) エ
(5) イ，ウ

解説

(1) 第 1 段落第 4 文から，ナバホ語は非常に複雑で，使いこなせる人がごく少ないことから，「戦場で重要な情報を安全に送るための解読不可能な暗号を作る」(create an unbreakable code … on the battlefields)ために使われたことがわかる。この目的を指定された字数で答える。

(2) 下線部②の This trend は，直前の第 2 段落第 2～3 文で述べている「傾向」，つまりアメリカ先住民の言語の中で最も話者人口が多いとされるナバホ語も，現在では日常的に使う人が急速に減っていることを指している。

(3) 空所③の前後が「ナバホ語を活性化することが急務であることを認識した」となるように，アの revitalize「～を活性化する」を選ぶ。イ suppress「～を抑圧する」，ウ disrupt「～を乱す，混乱させる」，エ ratify「～を批准する」では，どれも意味が通じない。

(4) 補う英文は，「何千人ものナバホ族がこの映画を楽しむ機会を得た」という意味。文末の the film は，第 4 段落第 4 文の The Navajo version of *Star Wars Episode IV* を指すので，このあとに続く[エ]の位置に入れるのが適切である。

(5) ア 選択肢の訳 「第二次世界大戦中，いくつかの複雑な言語に基づく暗号を解読するために，多くのナバホ語話者が徴用された」 第 1 段落第 3～4 文の内容と不一致。ナバホ語話者が徴用されたのは，「解読不可能な暗号を作る」(create an unbreakable code)ためであって，(敵側の)暗号を解読するためではない。 イ 選択肢の訳 「ナバホ語はアメリカ先住民の言語の中で最も話者人口が多い」第 2 段落第 4 文後半の has a larger number of speakers compared to many other Native American languages と一致。これが正解の 1 つ目。 ウ 選択肢の訳 「マヌエリート・ウィーラー氏は，『スター・ウォーズ エピソード 4』をナバホ族の母語に吹き替えれば，言語の保存に役立つかもしれないと考えた」 第 3 段落第 3 文の he thought … 以下の内容と一致。これが正解の 2 つ目。 エ 選択肢の訳 「その言語の複雑さのために，『ス

ター・ウォーズ』の脚本をナバホ語に翻訳するには膨大な時間がかかった」 第4段落第2文で The translation itself took only less than 40 hours と説明している内容と食い違う。 オ 選択肢の訳 「『スター・ウォーズ エピソード4』のナバホ語版DVDが発売されて以来，母語を学ぶナバホ族の若者の数が増えている」 第5段落の内容と不一致。ナバホ語版の『スター・ウォーズ エピソード4』がきっかけで，実際にナバホ語部族内に母語話者が増えたとは書かれていない。

<全訳>
ナバホ語
　アメリカ先住民の言語の1つであるナバホ語は，「ディネ ビザール」としても知られ，世界で最も複雑な言語の1つとして際立つ存在である。その複雑な構造と固有の特徴のために，習得するのが非常に難しい言語となっており，ほんの限られた数の人しか使いこなすことができない。その複雑さのために，ナバホ語は第二次世界大戦中に暗号として使われ，その際，多くのナバホ語話者が「コードトーカー」として米軍に徴用された。彼らは，戦場で重要な情報を安全に送るための解読不可能な暗号を作るために，母語を使うことによって米軍で重要な役割を果たした。
　今日，アメリカにはおよそ112のアメリカ先住民の言語が生き残っており，その多くは保留地と呼ばれるコミュニティの中で話されている。しかし，そのようなコミュニティにおいても，自分たちの言語を話すことができるアメリカ先住民の数は急速に減少している。ますます多くのアメリカ先住民が，家庭内においても母語の代わりに英語を使うようになっているのである。こうした傾向は，ほかの多くのアメリカ先住民の言語に比べて話者数の多いナバホ語にも当てはまる。
　ナバホ部族博物館の館長であるマヌエリート・ウィーラー氏は，ナバホ語を活性化させることが急務であることを認識し，革新的な解決策を模索した。1996年ごろ，ウィーラー氏は『スター・ウォーズ』映画シリーズの1つをナバホ語に吹き替えることを思いついた。ジョージ・ルーカス監督による『スター・ウォーズ』シリーズの熱狂的なファンであった彼は，ナバホ族の人々がナバホ語音声の入った大ヒット映画を楽しむことができれば，消滅の危機に瀕している言語を保存することにつながるだろうと考えたのである。

　ウィーラー氏は翻訳チームを作ると，『スター・ウォーズ エピソード4／新たなる希望』の脚本をナバホ語に翻訳する作業に取り組んだ。翻訳自体に要した時間はわずか40時間足らずであったが，映画製作会社との交渉はスムーズには進まなかった。ディズニーとルーカスフィルムがこの野心的なプロジェクトを支援することに同意したのは，2012年の春のことだった。ナバホ語版『スター・ウォーズ エピソード4』は，2012年のナバホ部族フェアで初公開され，その後，全米のさまざまなイベントで上映された。何千人ものナバホ族がこの映画を楽しむ機会を得た。
　2013年には，ナバホ語版の『スター・ウォーズ エピソード4』がDVDで発売された。ウィーラー氏は，このプロジェクトの成功がナバホ族の人々の誇りとなり，ナバホ族の若者たちが母語に興味を持つきっかけになることを願っている。

NOTE

NOTE

NOTE

Ambition English Communication Ⅲ
Workbook
解答・解説

BD

開隆堂出版株式会社
東京都文京区向丘1-13-1

Ambition

English Communication III

Workbook

開隆堂

本書の構成と使い方

このワークブックは，「Ambition English Communication Ⅲ」の内容に沿って作られています。教科書で扱われた Lesson 1 から 11 の重要表現と語いの理解に役立つ，さまざまな形式の問題で構成してあります。各 Lesson は，重要表現と語いの理解を目標とした基本問題，大学受験への橋渡しとなる発展問題から構成されています。また，巻末には教科書に掲載された熟語の一覧を掲載していますので，毎日の授業の予習だけでなく，復習や定期テスト前の整理にも役立ちます。各ページの内容と使い方は次のとおりです。

●基本問題

教科書各 Lesson のパートごとに問題を掲載しています。試験でよく問われる最頻出問題を厳選して紹介していますので予習に適しています。さまざまな出題形式から重要表現と語いを練習できるよう工夫しておりますので，定期テスト対策としても役立ちます。一度解いた問題も何回も音読すると定着も早く進みます。

●発展問題

大学受験への準備となるよう本課で扱った題材を別な視点から扱った長文問題を掲載しています。長文は本書用に書き下ろしたオリジナルなので，時間を計るなど試験のつもりで解くとよいでしょう。

目次

1 Choose the correct answer.

(1) The popularity of esports has grown (dramatically / dramatic) in recent years.

(2) The team won victories in two (categories / category).

(3) He participated in an (internationally / ironically) renowned chess championship.

(4) We (secretly / commonly) planned a surprise party for Emma.

2 Fill in the blanks to complete the sentences.

(1) ジェーンは日本の伝統文化に強い関心を持っています。

Jane has a (　　　　　) interest in traditional Japanese culture.

(2) 拍手喝采の音が劇場内に響き渡りました。

The sound of applause (　　　　　) throughout the theater.

(3) 若者たちに夢を追い求めるように勧めることは大切です。

It is important to (　　　　) young people (　　　　) pursue their dreams.

(4) 最終戦の模様を撮影したビデオ・ストリーミングは全世界に配信されました。

The video streaming of the final (　　　　　) was broadcast internationally.

3 Reorder the words in brackets so that they make sense.

(1) In the past, high blood pressure (to / commonly / as / referred / was) the "silent killer."

_____

(2) Athletes from all over the world (against / other / compete / each) at the Olympics.

_____

(3) This is a wooden box (Jane / which / used / keep / to / in) her jewels.

_____

(4) The boy (playing / keen / soccer / on / is).

_____

4 Translate the Japanese into English.

(1) そのアニメのイベントは2万5千人もの大観衆を呼び寄せました。

_____

(2) 彼女はそのパーティーで居心地の悪い思いをしました。

_____

(3) 賞金のためにプロとして(professionally)ビデオゲームをプレイする人たちもいます。

_____

(4) 梅原は世界的に有名なトーナメントの1つでチャンピオンになりました。

_____

1 Choose the correct answer.

(1) He made a big mistake at a (critical / critic) moment.

(2) She won the (championship / champion) in the competition.

(3) I used to (frequent / frequently) game arcades when I was a high school student.

(4) The pianist (skillfully / skillful) played the tune.

2 Fill in the blanks to complete the sentences.

(1) そのチームは試合中，たいへんな集中力を見せました。

The team showed great (　　　　　　) during the game.

(2) その不祥事に対する世間の反応はほとんど間を置かずに起きました。

Public reaction to the scandal was almost (　　　　　　).

(3) この世界は急速に変化しつつあり，私たちには最新の知識が要求されます。

The rapidly changing world requires us to have (　　　　　) knowledge.

(4) カナはそのテレビドラマの主人公に共感しました。

Kana (　　　　　　) with the main character of the TV drama.

3 Reorder the words in brackets so that they make sense.

(1) (invited / Kaori / was / dinner / to) at Adam's house.

_____

(2) The task was (expected / I / difficult / far / than / had / more).

_____

(3) He (of / spends / most / his free time / reading) mystery novels.

_____

(4) Masao can (English / speak / not / also / but / only) German.

_____

4 Translate the Japanese into English.

(1) 彼女は貧しい子どもたちを救うことに専念しました。

_____

(2) 彼女は自分の本当の力はほかのだれよりも速く走ることなのだとわかりました。

_____

(3) 私は海外留学中に多くの人と知り合いになりました。

_____

(4) 彼の小説は国の内外で非常に人気があります。(both を使って)

_____

1   Choose the correct answer.

(1) Katie is interested in movie (editing / edit) these days.

(2) I had a new air-conditioner (installed / attached) last week.

(3) The students were (enrolled / contained) in the new language course.

(4) An accident forced her (withdrawal / withdraw) from the competition.

2   Fill in the blanks to complete the sentences.

(1) 子どもがスマホ中毒となるリスクは常にあるのです。

There is always a risk that children will become (　　　　　) (　　　　　　) smartphones.

(2) サムは昼夜逆転した生活を送っています。

Sam spends his day-night (　　　　　) life.

(3) ビルは昇給を要求したものの拒否されました。

Bill faced a (　　　　　) when he asked for a raise at work.

(4) その会社は地元の大学と協力してその新製品を開発しました。

The company developed the new product in (　　　　　) (　　　　　) local universities.

3   Reorder the words in brackets so that they make sense.

(1) (allowed / you / to / are / take / not) pictures inside the building.

_____

(2) The students seem to be (communicating / enjoying / with / other / each).

_____

(3) You (to / ample / opportunity / share / have) your opinions.

_____

(4) This textbook (beginners / to / is / teach / designed) how to program.

_____

4   Translate the Japanese into English.

(1) 日本の人口の20パーセント以上は65歳を超えています。（～を超えて＝over）

_____

(2) 彼女は天文学に関する幅広い知識を持っています。

_____

(3) そのレストランではさまざまな種類の料理を楽しむことができます。（sort を使って）

_____

(4) あなたは1日に何時間ビデオゲームをプレイすることを練習しますか。

_____

■ Choose the correct answer.

(1) The professional gamer spends most of his time (honing / hone) his skills.

(2) Can we learn the skills of (logical / logic) thinking through playing games?

(3) The port city is located at a (strategically / strategy) important point.

(4) Their demand for a higher wage was refused (promptly / prompt).

■ Fill in the blanks to complete the sentences.

(1) 包丁の刃を研いでいただけますか。

Could you (　　　　　　　) the kitchen knife?

(2) 目標を達成したいのなら，目的意識を持って行動すべきです。

You should act (　　　　　　　) if you want to achieve your goals.

(3) 私たちはその問題についてあらゆる面から議論する必要があります。

We need to discuss the issue from all (　　　　　　　).

(4) 彼女はみんなの先に立ってそのチャリティーイベントを準備しました。

She took the (　　　　　　　) to organize the charity event.

■ Reorder the words in brackets so that they make sense.

(1) Esports players need to make quick decisions (to / win / order / competitive games / in).

_____

(2) We are allowed to stay in the building (half / one / and / a / hours / for only).

_____

(3) (needed / research / how / to / find out / is) the use of AI will help educate children.

_____

(4) Alice showed us how to cook tomatoes (grow / how / as / as / to / them / well).

_____

■ Translate the Japanese into English.

(1) 日本では公衆電話(public phones)の数が急激に減っています。

_____

(2) 来年はだれが美術部の担当者になるのでしょうか。

_____

(3) 彼は子どもがどのようにして言語を獲得するのかに興味があります。

_____

(4) 彼は新しいコースが学生たちの書く技術の向上に役立つことを期待しています。

_____

Mobile Gaming

Playing video games has become a popular activity in modern society. The global video game population is steadily increasing every year, and it is estimated that there are approximately 3.7 billion video gamers around the world as of 2023. The world's population is approximately 8 billion, so (　①　) speaking, nearly half of the world's population plays video games. As the world's video game population is increasing, so is the size of the video game industry. Now it makes more money than the sports and movie industries combined.

What is causing such an increase in the number of video gamers? No doubt, the widespread use of mobile devices is greatly contributing to ②it. In the past, many people might have associated video gamers with PCs or *game consoles. These days, however, the fastest-growing *segment of video gamers is shifting to mobile devices, especially smartphones. According to the latest study, about 70% of people prefer to play video games on smartphones. Game consoles come in second, with 52%, and PCs come in third, with 43%.

③One of the biggest reasons for mobile gaming's popularity is its accessibility. Now that a smartphone has become a common device, many people carry it anywhere anytime as if it were part of their body. They spend their *in-between time on trains or buses playing video games on their smartphones. Additionally, a wide range of mobile games are available, from *action-packed adventures to *brain-teasing puzzles, so people of different age groups can find their favorite games. It makes gaming an enjoyable experience for them.

During the COVID-19 pandemic, all gaming *platforms saw a business boom, but mobile gaming experienced the most significant growth. Due to ④the lockdowns, people were forced to spend a great deal of time at home. Ironically enough, playing mobile games provided them with an opportunity to socialize with other gamers remotely and escape from stress.　　　　　　　　　　　　　　　　　　　　　　　　(314 words)

注：game console　ゲーム機　　segment　区分　　in-between time　隙間時間
　　action-packed　多くのアクションが含まれる　　brain-teasing　頭を使う
　　platform　プラットフォーム（ゲームをプレイするハードウェアの種類）

(1) ①に入る語として正しいものを1つ選び，記号で答えなさい。

ア frankly イ generally ウ roughly エ promptly

(　　)

(2) 下線部②が指す内容を本文中のひと続きの英語8語でそのまま書きなさい。

_____

(3) 下線部③に関して，人々のどのような習慣がモバイル・ゲームの人気を高めているのか。35
〜40字程度の日本語で説明しなさい。

_____習慣。

(4) 下線部④の期間中に起きたことの説明となるように，(　　　　)を補い，日本文を完成させな
さい。

(　　　　　　　　　　　　　　　　　　)ことを余儀なくされた人々にとって，モバイル・ゲー
ムをプレイすることは，(　　　　　　　　　　　　　　　　)機会となった。

(5) 本文の内容と一致するものを1つ選び，記号で答えなさい。

ア In spite of the growing global video game population, the size of the video game
industry has not grown so remarkably.

イ These days, PCs are the least preferred choice among gamers, falling behind
smartphones and game consoles.

ウ One problem with mobile games is that all of them are designed to suit young people's
tastes.

エ During the COVID-19 pandemic, the mobile gaming industry experienced a decline in
its popularity due to the lockdowns.

1   Choose the correct answer.

(1) (Fishing / Fisheries) are a major industry in many Northern European countries.

(2) According to the rumor, the company is facing a financial (collapse / carcass).

(3) The group of scientists published their (findings / seeings) in a journal.

(4) Some medicine is (deprived / derived) from marine sources.

2   Fill in the blanks to complete the sentences.

(1) 彼はバケツで川から水をすくい上げました。

He (　　　　　) (　　　　　　　　) some water from the river with a bucket.

(2) ショーウィンドウの中にずらりと並んだケーキを見て少女は目を輝かせました。

The girl's eyes lit up when she saw an (　　　　　　　) of cakes in the showcase.

(3) その大型の台風はその地域に甚大な損害をもたらしました。

The big typhoon (　　　　　　) terrible damage (　　　　　　) the areas.

(4) その男性は警察に事故がどのようにして起きたのかを説明しました。

The man explained to the police how the accident (　　　　　　) (　　　　　　).

(5) 嵐が静まるまでに数時間かかりました。

It took several hours before the storm (　　　　　　) (　　　　　　).

3   Reorder the words in brackets so that they make sense.

(1) The tourism industry (contributions / makes / lot of / to / a) the local economy every year.

_____

(2) (bears / the salmon carcasses / in / by / result / discarded) nourishing the forests.

_____

(3) The endangered species will disappear (carefully / protected / unless / are / they).

_____

4   Translate the Japanese into English.

(1) 私たちは湖畔にあるその美しい村を訪れ,そこに1週間滞在しました。(関係副詞を使って)

_____

(2) その事件の真相を知る人はほとんどいません。

_____

(3) ジャーナリストとしての彼のキャリアは30年以上にもわたります。(span を使って)

_____

(4) マークは試験のために一生懸命に勉強し,その結果,彼はクラスで最高の得点を獲得しました。

(that 節を使って)

Mark studied very hard for the exam, and _____.

1   Choose the correct answer.

(1) We have food and water in (abundance / abundant).

(2) The database provides us with the nutrient (composed / composition) of major foods.

(3) The lion and the tiger belong to the same (genus / genius).

(4) Salmon are in the habit of returning to their (natal / natural) streams.

2   Fill in the blanks to complete the sentences.

(1) ツノメドリはその一生の大半を海で過ごします。

Puffins spend most of their lives (　　　　　) (　　　　　).

(2) 8に3をかけると24になります。

(　　　　　) 8 (　　　　　) 3 and you get 24.

(3) 庭に咲いている花は色も形もさまざまです。

The flowers in the garden (　　　　　) (　　　　　) color and size.

(4) ある種の鳥は冬になると暖かい地域に渡りをします。

Some bird species (　　　　　) to warmer regions in the winter.

(5) 野生動物の世界では，子どもたちは常に捕食者の脅威にさらされています。

In wild nature, (　　　　　) are always facing threats from their predators.

3   Reorder the words in brackets so that they make sense.

(1) The oil spill can (on / have / the marine ecosystem / a long-term effect).

_____

(2) (from / after / the gravel / emerging), young salmon swim toward the ocean.

_____

(3) Freshwater (1% / less / salt / of / than / contains).

_____

4   Translate the Japanese into English.

(1) 彼女には並外れた音楽の才能があります。

_____

(2) 1頭の乳牛は1日に平均24リットルのミルクを出します。(produce, an average を使って)

_____

(3) そのトカゲ(lizard)は体重が150キログラムにもなります。(weigh を使って)

_____

(4) 雨が激しく降っていましたが，エマは買い物を続けました。

_____

1　Choose the correct answer.

(1)　Does he always have such an (aggressive / aggregate) attitude?

(2)　Many (hibernators / hibernations) spend most of the winter months in their dens.

(3)　The other part of the (equal / equation) is providing first-class customer service.

(4)　How do animals increase their (reproductive / reproduce) success?

2　Fill in the blanks to complete the sentences.

(1)　その国の多くの子どもは(文字を)読むことも書くこともできません。

　　　Many children in the country can (　　　　　　) read (　　　　　　) write.

(2)　羊は牧草地の草を常食としています。

　　　Sheep (　　　　　　) (　　　　　　) grass in the meadow.

(3)　その計画の成功はメンバー同士の明確なコミュニケーションにかかっています。

　　　The success of the project (　　　　　) (　　　　　) clear communication among members.

(4)　私たちはそのレストランで豪華な料理を楽しみました。

　　　We (　　　　　　) (　　　　　　) gorgeous dishes at the restaurant.

3　Reorder the words in brackets so that they make sense.

(1)　My sister (a baby girl / to / gave / birth) last week.

_____

(2)　Natural selection (nourishment / that / favors / the most / get / those).

_____

(3)　Reading an English newspaper is (to / your English / a good way / improve).

_____

(4)　Hibernating animals (survive / deposit / fat / enough / to) the winter.

_____

4　Translate the Japanese into English.

(1)　石油はあらゆる産業にとって極めて重要な資源です。

_____

(2)　健康はバランスのとれた(balanced)食事や十分な睡眠と密接に関わっています。

_____

(3)　計画も目標もなしに何かを始めることは時間の無駄に終わる可能性があります。

　　　　　　　　　　　　　　　　　　　　　　　　(result 動を使って)

_____

(4)　ジャックはひとたび勉強し始めると，何時間もそれに集中します。

_____

1 Choose the correct answer.

(1) She (selectively / selective) chose the best flowers from the garden.

(2) What is the population (density / dense) of your city?

(3) I saw crows (scavenging / scavenger) garbage on the sidewalk.

(4) The (decomposed / decompose) carcass of a whale was washed up at the beach.

2 Fill in the blanks to complete the sentences.

(1) エマはあまりにも疲れていたので，夕食を一口も食べずに寝てしまいました。

Emma was so tired that she went to bed without eating (   ) (   ) of
dinner.

(2) その豪雨の中で，川の汚染物質はすべて海に流されてしまいました。

During the heavy rain, all the pollutants in the river were (   ) (   )
into the ocean.

(3) 結局のところ，私たちは明日何が起こるかを予想できないのです。

(   ) (   ), we cannot tell what will happen tomorrow.

(4) スマートフォンはそれなしには不可能であろうインターネットへの容易なアクセスを提
供してくれます。

Smartphones provide us with easy access to the Internet that (   ) not
(   ) be possible.

3 Reorder the words in brackets so that they make sense.

(1) The country (fresh water / has / available / made) for everyone.

_____

(2) The bus left the terminal (of / not occupied / with / the seats / most).

_____

(3) Many people buy (than / far / eat / food / they / more / can).

_____

4 Translate the Japanese into English.

(1) 以前は日本人が朝食にごはんを食べるのはふつうのことでした。

_____

(2) 現代の車に比べて，古い車はより多くのガソリンを消費します。（compared to を使って）

_____

(3) 彼がコンピュータをセットアップするのに1時間もかかりませんでした。

_____

13

The Great Bear Rainforest

The word "rainforests" may remind you of ①those that exist in tropical zones closer to the *equator. Tropical forests are a *hotspot of biodiversity and are believed to be home to approximately 80% of the world's documented species. Not only that, but they also play a crucial role in *regulating the global climate by *sequestering large amounts of carbon dioxide and releasing water through a process called *evapotranspiration. However, not many people know about another type of rainforest called *temperate rainforests, which also play an important role in regulating the global climate.

②Temperate rainforests are located in the mid-latitudes between the equator and polar regions, where temperatures are much milder than in the tropics. They are found mostly in coastal, mountainous areas, and due to these *geographical conditions, temperate rainforests experience significant rainfall throughout the year. The Great Bear Rainforest on the Pacific coast of British Columbia, Canada, is the largest coastal temperate rainforest in the world. From an ecological point of view, the Great Bear Rainforest is especially important because its ecosystem has relied on spawning salmon for its vitality for thousands of years.

There are more than 2,000 streams and rivers throughout the Great Bear Rainforest, and they function as a water network that connects the entire rainforest. Additionally, these *gravel-bed streams and rivers provide essential spawning grounds for Pacific salmon. Every year, millions of Pacific salmon return to these waters to spawn. These spawning salmon are a precious source of food for many animal species living in the rainforest, including bears, wolves, and eagles. These predators often bring the salmon they have caught to the forests to eat without interference from other predators. The salmon carcasses left in the forests are often eaten by scavengers, and then they decompose into fertilizer for the forests. ③In this way, spawning salmon continue to contribute to the forest ecosystem even after death.

The Great Bear Rainforest teaches us how the ecosystems on Earth are connected to each other in a complicated and unexpected manner. Every ecosystem has its own unique features, but they cannot exist alone. Efforts to safeguard the environment should be based on ④the idea that the entire Earth consists of one large ecosystem made up of smaller ones.

(375 words)

14

注：equator　赤道
　　　hotspot　ホットスポット（多数の絶滅危惧種が生息する，生物学的に特別な場所）
　　　regulate　～を正常に保つ　　sequester　隔離する　　evapotranspiration　蒸発散
　　　temperate　温帯の　　geographical　地理的な　　gravel-bed　河床が砂礫質の

(1)　下線部①が指す内容を本文中の英語1語で答えなさい。

　　　　　　　　　　　　　　　　　　　　　　　　　　　　＿＿＿＿＿＿＿＿＿＿＿＿＿

(2)　下線部②の説明となるように，（　　　　　）を補い，日本文を完成させなさい。
　　（　　　　　　　　　　　　　　　　　　　　　　　　　）の中緯度地方に位置し，その気温は
　　（　　　　　　　　　　　　　　　　　　　　　）である。主に海岸沿いの山岳地帯に分布し，
　　（　　　　　　　　　　　　　　　　　　　　　）。

(3)　下線部③に関して，グレート・ベア・レインフォレストに生息する捕食動物たちのどのよう
　　な行動がこのような結果を生むのか。40字程度の日本語で説明しなさい。

　　＿＿＿＿＿＿＿＿＿＿＿＿＿＿＿＿＿＿＿＿＿＿＿＿＿＿＿＿＿＿＿＿＿＿＿こと。

(4)　下線部④が表す考え方を簡潔に述べている箇所を本文から探し，ひと続きの英語13語でそ
　　のまま書きなさい。

　　＿＿＿＿＿＿＿＿＿＿＿＿＿＿＿＿＿＿＿＿＿＿＿＿＿＿＿＿＿＿＿＿＿＿＿＿＿

(5)　本文の内容と一致するものを2つ選び，記号で答えなさい。
　ア　It is estimated that about 80% of the world's species that have ever been discovered
　　　live in temperate forests.
　イ　The Great Bear Rainforest is one of the largest tropical rainforests on Earth.
　ウ　Temperate rainforests help regulate the global climate just as tropical rainforests do.
　エ　The ecosystem of the Great Bear Rainforest depends heavily on spawning salmon.
　オ　The Great Bear Rainforest shows us how each of the ecosystems on Earth exists
　　　independently.

1   Choose the correct answer.

(1)   The company is famous as a (producer / production) of organic vegetables.

(2)   Weather patterns differ between (inland / indoors) and coastal areas.

(3)   Several illegal street vendors were caught in the (crackup / crackdown).

(4)   The scandal was widely (publicized / public) in newspapers.

2   Fill in the blanks to complete the sentences.

(1)   その容疑者は警察に連行されて尋問を受けました。

The suspect was (   ) (   ) by police for questioning.

(2)   地元のサッカーチームはその有能な若者たちがチームに入るのを歓迎しました。

The local soccer team welcomed the talented (   ) to join them.

(3)   そのやせこけた男は手をもみ合わせながら答えました。

The (   ) man answered, (   ) his hands.

(4)   食品会社はより環境に優しい梱包を求める消費者からの増加しつつある要求に直面しています。

Food companies face (   ) (   ) from consumers for more eco-friendly packaging.

3   Reorder the words in brackets so that they make sense.

(1)   These products (of / are / harmful chemicals / any / free).

_____

(2)   The Midwest region is often (the heartland / as / America / referred to / of).

_____

(3)   Many children (to / were / the cocoa plantation / on / forced / work).

_____

4   Translate the Japanese into English.

(1)   一部の消費者は倫理的な製品を買うことを選びます。

_____

(2)   地域社会の役に立とうと多くの学生がボランティア活動に参加しています。

(involved を使って)

_____

(3)   コートジボワール (the Ivory Coast) は高品質のカカオ豆の生産国として知られています。

_____

(4)   一部の開発途上国では児童労働が日常的に行われています。(動詞に practice を使って)

_____

1　Choose the correct answer.

(1)　The (rider / riding) controlled his motorcycle skillfully.

(2)　The military (convey / convoy) moved slowly along the road.

(3)　The police conducted a sudden (swoop / hamlet) on the suspected gang hideout.

2　Fill in the blanks to complete the sentences.

(1)　その国の政府は緊急事態に対応するために部隊を動員しました。

The country's government (　　　　　　) troops to respond to the emergency.

(2)　両親はパーティーに出席している間，子どもたちをベビーシッターに預けました。

The parents (　　　　　) their children (　　　　　　) a babysitter while attending the
party.

(3)　その生徒は質問すべてに正しく答えることができました。

The student was (　　　　　) (　　　　　　) answer all the questions correctly.

(4)　彼はかごの中の洗濯物の山を見てため息をつきました。

He sighed at the (　　　　　) (　　　　　　) laundry in the basket.

(5)　プレゼンテーションの前に短い紹介があります。

A brief introduction will (　　　　　) the presentation.

3　Reorder the words in brackets so that they make sense.

(1)　The woman (the guest of honor / was / as / presented) at the event.

_____

(2)　Police officers (seen / were / the streets / roaming) in the city.

_____

(3)　(the case / if / is / you / for / this), we can arrange a different time to meet.

_____

4　Translate the Japanese into English.

(1)　その工場は天然ゴムを原料にしたさまざまな製品を製造しています。

_____

(2)　マサトは毎日バイクで通勤しています。

_____

(3)　ミナはスーパーマーケットで卵を1ダース買いました。

_____

(4)　人形博物館は，このような種類の博物館としては日本で唯一のものです。

_____

1　Choose the correct answer.

(1)　The hotel's (receive / reception) area was crowded with guests.

(2)　The family enjoyed spending weekends in the peaceful (countryside / countrywide).

(3)　How can (psychologists / psychological) support students' mental health?

(4)　The school announced a special discount for early (enroll / enrollment) in the course.

2　Fill in the blanks to complete the sentences.

(1)　ミカの家族は保護猫を引き取ることにしました。

　　Mika's family decided to (　　　　　　) (　　　　　　) a shelter cat.

(2)　その少年は両親が迎えに来るまで交番で待っていました。

　　The boy waited at the police station until his parents arrived to (　　　　　) him
　　(　　　　　).

(3)　政府は違法な森林伐採との闘いにおいて新たな作戦を始めました。

　　The government launched a new campaign in the (　　　　　) (　　　　　) illegal
　　deforestation.

(4)　勉強のかたわら，アランは自由時間にギターを弾いて楽しみます。

　　(　　　　　) (　　　　　) studying, Alan enjoys playing the guitar in his free time.

3　Reorder the words in brackets so that they make sense.

(1)　The construction work (being / out / by / carried / is) a team of skilled engineers.

　　―――――――――――――――――――――――――――――――――――――

(2)　Her grandmother (her / taught / of / sewing / the skill).

　　―――――――――――――――――――――――――――――――――――――

(3)　He learned the art of gardening and (it / trade / made / his).

　　―――――――――――――――――――――――――――――――――――――

4　Translate the Japanese into English.

(1)　一部の国々では，かなり多くの数の大人が字を読み書きできません。

　　　　　　　　　　　　　　　　　　　　　　　　　　　　　　（significant を使って）

　　―――――――――――――――――――――――――――――――――――――

(2)　毎年多くの幼児虐待の事例が報告されています。

　　―――――――――――――――――――――――――――――――――――――

(3)　彼らは2時間働いたあとで休憩を取るように言われました。（名詞の work を使って）

　　―――――――――――――――――――――――――――――――――――――

(4)　思春期の若者の心理を理解することはしばしば難しいです。

　　―――――――――――――――――――――――――――――――――――――

■ Choose the correct answer.

(1) Many Africans were (enslaved / slavery) on the plantations in the Caribbean region.

(2) The security cameras provide constant (surveillance / oversee) of the building.

(3) Let's ask a lawyer about how to take (legal / legally) action against the company.

■ Fill in the blanks to complete the sentences.

(1) 裁判官はその窃盗犯に懲役 5 年の判決を言い渡しました。

The judge (　　　　　　) the thief (　　　　　　) five years in prison.

(2) 児童売買の罪で 5 人の男が有罪判決を受けました。

Five men were (　　　　　　) of child (　　　　　　).

(3) その地域に住む多くの家庭が貧困ラインを下回る生活をしています。

Many families in the region live (　　　　) the (　　　　) (　　　　).

(4) その地域では，多くの人々が農業で生計を立てています。

In those areas, many people (　　　　) (　　　　) farming.

(5) 検察はその被告に懲役 3 年を求刑しました。

The (　　　　) demanded three years' (　　　　) for the accused.

■ Reorder the words in brackets so that they make sense.

(1) (the students / half / more / of / than) attended the event.

_____

(2) The case (court / was / to / brought).

_____

(3) The annual survey (conducted / 2010 / has / since / been).

_____

■ Translate the Japanese into English.

(1) このコースは学生たちのプレゼンテーションの技術を向上させることを目的にしています。（aim 動 を使って）

_____

(2) 未成年者の飲酒は法律により禁止されています。（prohibit を使って）

_____

(3) その少年はうそをついたために罰を受けました。

_____

(4) 多くの小さな会社は経済的な余裕がないために新しいコンピュータの購入を断念します。

_____

Growing Cocoa Demand

Global demand for chocolate is growing rapidly. Chocolate is mainly consumed in developed countries and is loved by people who want to relax by eating sweets. These days, chocolate consumption is rapidly increasing in *emerging countries（ ① ）. Particularly in India and China, the chocolate market is growing faster as more and

5　more people turn to chocolate for special moments.

The problem is that cocoa beans, one of the main ingredients in chocolate production, don't naturally grow just anywhere on Earth. Cocoa trees need hot and humid weather with ample rain to grow well, so they are cultivated only in tropical areas, within 20 degrees north and south of the *equator. Often called the cocoa belt, the region stretches

10　from Central and West Africa, Indonesia, to Central and South America. In fact, more than 90 percent of the world's cocoa comes from the developing countries located in these areas. The world's two largest cocoa producers are specifically *Côte d'Ivoire, or the Ivory Coast, and *Ghana. These two West African countries alone account for more than half of the world's cocoa production. ②That means even a minor decline in cocoa

15　*harvest in these two countries can significantly affect the global cocoa market.

③In recent years, a considerable number of cocoa farmers have been forced to give up growing cocoa trees. Due to global climate change, many cocoa-producing countries don't have proper amounts of rain for cocoa trees to grow normally. To make matters worse, as climate change continues, it has weakened cocoa trees' ability to fight diseases

20　and *pests. As a result, many cocoa trees are dying, leading to a ④decrease in cocoa production.

In the face of such a critical situation, many cocoa farmers cannot afford to take effective measures. Some major chocolate manufacturers worldwide are engaging in projects to preserve cocoa farms and *revitalize cocoa production. However, the

25　increasing pace of chocolate demand *outstrips the progress of these *initiatives.

(323 words)

注：emerging countries　新興国　　equator　赤道
　　Côte d'Ivoire　コートジボワール（英名 the Ivory Coast）
　　Ghana　ガーナ（コートジボワールの東隣の国）　　harvest　収穫（量）　　pest　害虫
　　revitalize　～を復興させる，再生する　　outstrip　～を上回る
　　initiative　新たな取り組み

(1) ①に入る語句として正しいものを1つ選び，記号で答えなさい。

ア　as well　　イ　here and there　　ウ　each other　　エ　for short

（　　　）

(2) 下線部②の具体的内容となるように，（　　　）を補い，日本文を完成させなさい。

コートジボワールとガーナという（　　　　　　　　　　　　　　　　　　　　　）だ
けで（　　　　　　　　　　　　　　　　　　　　　　）を占めていること。

(3) 下線部③に関して，地球規模の気候変動は，どのような面でカカオ栽培に影響を及ぼしているのか。本文中のひと続きの英語(10語以内)で2つ答えなさい。

・＿＿＿＿＿＿＿＿＿＿＿＿＿＿＿＿＿＿＿＿＿＿＿＿＿＿＿＿＿

・＿＿＿＿＿＿＿＿＿＿＿＿＿＿＿＿＿＿＿＿＿＿＿＿＿＿＿＿＿

(4) 下線部④とほぼ同じ意味で用いられている英語1語を本文中から探して答えなさい。

＿＿＿＿＿＿＿＿＿＿＿＿＿＿

(5) 本文の内容と一致するものを2つ選び，記号で答えなさい。

ア　Both India and China are considering producing cocoa beans to meet the increasing demand for chocolate.

イ　The global cocoa market can easily be affected by the decline in harvest in the two tropical developing countries.

ウ　The world's largest cocoa producers are located in South America because it provides the best weather for growing cocoa trees.

エ　Some cocoa farmers are seeking help from scientists to deal with the diseases and pests affecting their cocoa trees.

オ　Many cocoa farms are giving up growing cocoa trees because they are more likely to be affected by climate change.

Part 1　基本問題

1　Choose the correct answer.

(1)　We planted new flowers to (rejuvenate / juvenile) the garden.

(2)　The (immigration / immigrant) officer asked for my passport.

(3)　Our (objective / objection) in the game is to score as many goals as possible.

(4)　The queen's daughter will become the next queen in (succeed / succession).

2　Fill in the blanks to complete the sentences.

(1)　そのテニスの選手は世界ランキング第4位です。

The tennis player (　　　　　) (　　　　　) in the world.

(2)　観光客の間で最も人気のある目的地はスペインで, イタリアとギリシャがそれに続きます。

The most popular destination among tourists is Spain, (　　　　　) (　　　　　) Italy and Greece.

(3)　彼らは技能実習生として実用的な技術を学んでいます。

They are learning practical skills as (　　　　　) (　　　　　) (　　　　　).

(4)　色に関して言えば, 青が私の好みです。

(　　　　　) (　　　　　) of colors, blue is my favorite.

3　Reorder the words in brackets so that they make sense.

(1)　He (as / as / is / a singer / not / but / regarded) an actor.

_____

(2)　(how / hours / the statistics / many / show) a day people sleep.

_____

(3)　The number of schools in our city (that / half of / is / than / less) in the neighboring cities.

_____

4　Translate the Japanese into English.

(1)　日本の学校では, 生徒は毎日教室を掃除するように期待されています。(expect を使って)

_____

(2)　多くの国が出生率の低下に直面しています。(face 動を使って)

_____

(3)　適量のチョコレートを食べることは健康によいと主張されています。(argue を使って)

_____

(4)　雨のために私たちはサイクリングに行けませんでした。

_____

22

1 Choose the correct answer.

(1) Today many countries (utilize / utility) sunlight as a renewable source of energy.

(2) (Except for / Except) swimming, Jessica enjoys all sports.

(3) The class reunion was a great time to (social / socialize) with my old friends.

2 Fill in the blanks to complete the sentences.

(1) 金沢は小京都として知られています。

Kanazawa is (   ) (   ) 'Little Kyoto.'

(2) 日本は外国から大量の食料を輸入しています。

Japan imports (   ) (   ) of food from overseas.

(3) 現在の駅ビルは 1980 年代に建てられました。

The current station building was (   ) (   ) in the 1980s.

(4) その会社は潤沢な予算のおかげで，すべてのコンピュータを買い換えることができました。

The company's (   ) (   ) allowed them to replace all the computers.

(5) その公園はショッピングモールの近くにあります。

The park is located in the (   ) (   ) the shopping mall.

3 Reorder the words in brackets so that they make sense.

(1) Many workers (big cities / move / higher wages / to / for).

_____

(2) They (to / paid / intermediary agencies / some money) for a work permit.

_____

(3) He got (clear off / money / enough / his debt / to / all).

_____

4 Translate the Japanese into English.

(1) その少年は野球のグローブを買うためにできるだけたくさんのお金をためました。

_____

(2) 高齢のため，私の祖父はめったに家から外に出ません。

_____

(3) 毎年多くの観光客がその伝統文化を体験するために日本にやってきます。

_____

(4) その施設は博物館だけでなく劇場も備えています。（house 動を使って）

_____

1 Choose the correct answer.

(1) Maria and Ron were chosen as the (represents / representatives) of their class.

(2) Should we accept more foreign (labors / laborers)?

(3) You need to pay a membership (fee / fare) to join the club.

2 Fill in the blanks to complete the sentences.

(1) エマは新入生でしたが，あっという間に新しい友だちができました。

Emma was a (　　　　　) to our school, but she quickly made new friends.

(2) そのチームは出身校が異なる選手たちで構成されています。

The team is (　　　　) (　　　　　) players from different schools.

(3) 私たちが新しい家に落ち着くにはまだ数日かかるでしょう。

It will take us another few days to (　　　　) (　　　　　) our new home.

(4) 暑い夏の間，水不足に悩まされる地域もあります。

During the hot summer, some places (　　　　) (　　　　) a shortage of water.

(5) 先生は研究活動のためにクラスを4つのグループに分けました。

The teacher (　　　　) the class (　　　　) four groups for the research activity.

3 Reorder the words in brackets so that they make sense.

(1) In Japan, we (clean water / take / a matter of course / getting / as).

_____

(2) My little sister (shopping / insisted / going / on) with me.

_____

(3) They (hard / learn / are / to / struggling) how to read and write.

_____

4 Translate the Japanese into English.

(1) 彼らは議論において合意点を見出すことができませんでした。（fail to を使って）

_____

(2) チームメイトの間には相互の理解が必要です。

_____

(3) 私に関して言えば，いつも環境に優しい製品を選ぶようにしています。

_____

(4) 彼らはいっしょに過ごす時間が増えるにつれて，文化の違いを乗り越えました。

_____

1　Choose the correct answer.

(1)　Some foreign workers acquire the (status / statue) of permanent residents.

(2)　Read carefully through the (term / terms) of the contract before you sign it.

(3)　You can choose either chicken (or / and) pork for the lunch menu.

2　Fill in the blanks to complete the sentences.

(1)　その両親は子どもたちのために何でもしようと決心しました。

The parents decided to do anything (　　　　　) their children's (　　　　　).

(2)　その施設は国籍に関係なく，だれでも利用することができます。

The facility is open for use by anyone, (　　　　) (　　　　) (　　　　).

(3)　アンは歴史のレポートをわずか3時間で書き上げました。

Anne finished writing her history report in no (　　　　) (　　　　) three hours.

(4)　だれもが彼のことを正直だと思っていたが，実際はそうではありませんでした。

Everyone had believed he was honest, but (　　　　) (　　　　) he was not.

(5)　多くの人々がその法律は改正されるべきだと考えています。

Many people believe the law should (　　　　) (　　　　).

3　Reorder the words in brackets so that they make sense.

(1)　The software (digital images / users / enables / edit / to).

_____

(2)　The new road will (it / go / make / to / possible) to the tourist attraction faster.

_____

(3)　The school will (for / expand / new students / the acceptance quota) next year.

_____

4　Translate the Japanese into English.

(1)　ユキは来月カイトと結婚することになっています。

_____

(2)　その図書館では一度に3冊まで本を借りることができます。（allow 動を使って）

_____

(3)　その家族は日本に永住することを選びました。（permanent 形を使って）

_____

(4)　気候変動は世界中の食料生産に影響を及ぼすと予想されています。（expected を使って）

_____

'When in Rome'

An old *saying *goes, 'When in Rome, do as the Romans do.' This saying emphasizes that when we are in a foreign land, we should adapt to the customs and traditions of the local people. Its origins can *be traced back to the 4th century A.D. during the Roman Empire. Even today, the *proverb is so widely recognized that simply saying 'when in
5 Rome' *conveys ①its meaning. However, the true challenge *lies in practicing its advice.

In reality, people from the same country often gather and form their own communities within foreign countries. For instance, Chinatowns or Korean towns are common in various parts of the world. Similarly, Japanese people living overseas tend to flock together instead of mixing with the local people. In today's digital age, such
10 patterns of 'gathering together' can become even stronger. One of the significant *factors contributing to ②this trend is language *barriers.

These days, a considerable number of foreigners come to Japan to find a job or acquire skills in various fields. They are expected to provide valuable *human resources to Japan, which has been struggling with a shortage of workers. However, *workplaces
15 that accept foreign workers often face a mutual understanding gap due to language barriers. These barriers prevent foreign workers from （ ③ ） Japanese colleagues or local residents near their residences, offices, or factories. Also, some foreign workers don't follow Japanese customs, and they create their own groups and prefer their own styles.

20 Considering Japan's declining birthrate, the country will need to increasingly rely on foreign labor in the near future. ［ア］ *Effective communication is essential for mutual understanding in the workplace, and language is at its core. ［イ］ At the same time, people from different places can learn to understand each other better by working together to find common ground. ［ウ］ For hosts, it is very important that they provide
25 an environment where foreign workers can adapt to Japanese customs and traditions while showing what they're good at. ［エ］ On the other hand, foreign workers may need to make a conscious effort to understand and follow Japanese rules and customs.

(357 words)

注：saying ことわざ，格言   go ～と言っている
　　be traced back to ～ ～にさかのぼる   proverb ことわざ
　　convey ～を伝える   lie in ～ ～にある   factor 要因

barrier　障害，障壁　　human resources　人材，人的資源
workplace　職場，仕事場　　effective　効果的な

(1)　下線部①に関して，文頭に挙げられている古いことわざは，何をすることの重要性を述べているのか。本文中のひと続きの英語10語で答えなさい。

　　_____

(2)　下線部②は，具体的にはどのような傾向のことか。本文の内容に即して，日本語で簡潔に説明しなさい。

　　_____傾向。

(3)　③に入る語句として正しいものを1つ選び，記号で答えなさい。
　　ア　fighting against　　　イ　interacting with
　　ウ　taking part in　　　　エ　refraining from

　　　　　　　　　　　　　　　　　　　　　　　　　　　　　（　　　）

(4)　以下の英文を補うのに適切な位置を，文中のア～エから選び，記号で答えなさい。
　　It enables them to get over language barriers.

　　　　　　　　　　　　　　　　　　　　　　　　　　　　　（　　　）

(5)　本文の内容と一致するものを2つ選び，記号で答えなさい。
　　ア　The old saying teaches us how ancient Roman people lived, respecting each other.
　　イ　Chinatowns are a good example of how well people can adapt to the local customs.
　　ウ　People of the same nationality often form their own communities in foreign countries.
　　エ　Not all foreign workers are getting along well with their Japanese colleagues and local people.
　　オ　In order to get a job in Japan, foreign workers need to acquire the ability to communicate in Japanese.

1　Choose the correct answer.

(1)　The actor has a (charismatic / charisma) personality.

(2)　Emma is (whole / wholly) devoted to teaching.

(3)　Steve Jobs was a (visionary / vision) who created a lot of innovative products.

(4)　All of the flowers arranged on the dishes are (endurable / edible).

2　Fill in the blanks to complete the sentences.

(1)　その学校のカリキュラムは数学，科学，美術などの科目を含みます。

　　The school's (　　　　　　　) includes subjects like math, science, and art.

(2)　農民たちは畑から農作物を収穫しました。

　　The farmers (　　　　　　　) crops from their fields.

(3)　その家族は家庭菜園にさまざまな種をまきました。

　　The family (　　　　　　) a variety of (　　　　　　) in their vegetable garden.

(4)　私たちの使命はプラスチックごみに関する人々の意識を高めることです。

　　Our (　　　　　　) is to raise people's awareness about plastic waste.

(5)　都市に樹木を植えることは環境の観点から見て好ましいです。

　　Planting trees in cities is good from an (　　　　　　) viewpoint.

3　Reorder the words in brackets so that they make sense.

(1)　She (with / beautified / flowers / her room / a lot of).

_____

(2)　The science teacher (an interesting experiment / involved / in / the students).

_____

(3)　We should (way / realize / the / affects / daily food) our health.

_____

4　Translate the Japanese into English.

(1)　動物園はいろいろな種類の動物を見ることができる場所です。(which を使って)

_____

(2)　ポールは仕事の行き帰りに本を読みます。

_____

(3)　ジェーンは将来の計画に対する両親の反応にうろたえました。(feel dismay を使って)

_____

(4)　よく眠れるように寝る前に音楽を聞く人もいます。

_____

1　Choose the correct answer.

(1)　It will be about a week before the seed (germinates / generates) in the soil.

(2)　The old house will be (refurbished / refurbishing) to make it look new and modern.

(3)　The beautiful sunset was an (inspiring / inspiration) for the young artist's painting.

2　Fill in the blanks to complete the sentences.

(1)　その古い廃棄された建物は見苦しい状態でした。

　　　The old, abandoned building was in an (　　　　　　) state.

(2)　メアリーは手紙を読んだあとで，それを破りました。

　　　Mary (　　　　　　) (　　　　　　) the letter after reading it.

(3)　そのアプリケーションには AI ツールが組み込まれています。

　　　AI tools are (　　　　　　) (　　　　　　) the application.

(4)　細菌を洗い流すために定期的に手を洗わなければなりません。

　　　You must wash your hands regularly to (　　　　　　) them of germs.

(5)　その教師は学ぶことに対する情熱を生徒たちに植え付けました。

　　　The teacher (　　　　　　) a (　　　　　　) for learning in his students.

3　Reorder the words in brackets so that they make sense.

(1)　(has / the company / a major sponsor / remained /) of the event since it started.

　　　_____

(2)　(to / purchase / the grant / the school / allowed) new computers.

　　　_____

(3)　He completed his task (the schedule / without / affected / being) by the accident.

　　　_____

4　Translate the Japanese into English.

(1)　持続可能な社会を実現するために私たちは一人一人が自分の役割を果たすべきです。

　　　_____

(2)　プロジェクトの成功はさまざまな要因に左右されます。

　　　_____

(3)　市はその使われていない施設を活用する方法を探しています。

　　　_____

(4)　アスファルトの道路は簡単に短時間で建設できます。

　　　_____

1 Choose the correct answer.

(1) The trainees need (hands-on / hand-on) experience with the equipment.

(2) I spread some (masturd / mustard) on my sandwich to add flavor.

(3) The factory increased its (output / outcome) of toys to meet the high demand.

(4) If you (compost / compose) food scraps in the garden, it will help your plants grow better.

2 Fill in the blanks to complete the sentences.

(1) この図書館では訪問者は求める本を棚から直接とることができます。

In this library, visitors can take the books they want (　　　　　) (　　　　　) the shelves.

(2) 猫はだれにも気付かれずにこっそりと出て行きました。

The cat sneaked away (　　　　　) (　　　　　) noticed by anyone.

(3) 私たちは数頭のシカが公園を歩いているのを見ました。

We saw several (　　　　　) walking in the park.

(4) 少年たちは芝生の上に腰を下ろし，サンドイッチをむしゃむしゃと食べました。

The boys sat on the grass and (　　　　　) (　　　　　) sandwiches.

3 Reorder the words in brackets so that they make sense.

(1) The children (the park / were / playing / in / out) all afternoon.

_____

(2) (what / good / eating / tastes) will make you happy.

_____

(3) (reason / should / there / no / we / is) put up with his rude manner.

_____

4 Translate the Japanese into English.

(1) すべての学生は英語のほかに外国語をもう1つ学ぶように奨励されます。

_____

(2) 私は母親が彼のことをキョンと呼ぶ男の子と仲良しです。

_____

(3) つまらないことにあなたの貴重な時間を無駄にするのはやめなさい。

_____

(4) 京都はエマが日本を旅行中に最初に訪れた場所でした。

_____

1　Choose the correct answer.

(1)　Fruits and vegetables are (nutrition / nutritious) foods that are good for our health.

(2)　You need (ingredient / ingredients) like flour, sugar, and eggs to make a delicious cake.

(3)　The team discussed their game (strategy / strategic) to win the soccer match.

2　Fill in the blanks to complete the sentences.

(1)　彼らはガーデン・セッションをカリキュラムの一部にしました。

They made the garden (　　　　　　　) part of the curriculum.

(2)　トムは昼休みとても忙しかったので，ハンバーガーを大急ぎで食べました。

Tom was so busy during lunchtime that he grabbed a hamburger (　　　　　　　) the (　　　　　).

(3)　その教師は学びを楽しくするために授業にゲームを持ち込みました。

The teacher (　　　　　　) a game (　　　　　　) his class to make learning fun.

(4)　最初，マキは地元のイタリア人たちとどう付き合えばよいのかわかりませんでした。

(　　　　　) (　　　　　　　　), Maki didn't know how to socialize with the local Italians.

3　Reorder the words in brackets so that they make sense.

(1)　The students did an experiment to (with / grow / see / plants / faster / sunlight / if).

_____

(2)　Some of our ideas (the new product / were / into / incorporated).

_____

(3)　The smell of freshly baked cookies (trying / anyone / them / seduces / into).

_____

4　Translate the Japanese into English.

(1)　大部分の家庭は限られた予算で家計をやりくりしなければなりません。

_____

(2)　私たちは夕食前にテーブルに新しいテーブルクロスを広げました。(spread を使って)

_____

(3)　暑い夏を乗り切る(beat)ための何かよいレシピを知っていますか。

_____

(4)　カズオは朝早く起きることに慣れています。

_____

Alice Waters

The Edible Schoolyard Project was established in 1995 by Alice Waters, a pioneer of the local food movement known for 'California cuisine.' Martin Luther King Jr. Middle School in *Berkeley, California, where the first seeds of the project were planted, is a ①'salad bowl' learning environment. Children from diverse cultural and economic backgrounds *come together at the school, and food serves as a common language that brings them together. Alice Waters *pioneered the concept of 'edible education,' and she put it into practice through the Edible Schoolyard Project. Its mission is to help students realize the connection between food and the land it comes from, which agrees with the principle of the local food movement she has advocated.

What is the background of Alice Waters' food movement? Waters says she had a keen sense of taste even when she was a little girl. However, what led her to the food movement was ②her experience studying in France during her university years. While staying in France in 1965, she was impressed by the small, family-owned restaurants *scattered across the country, as well as the local markets where people enjoyed shopping every day. The fresh ingredients people bought from the markets were cooked at home and shared with their families. For young Alice, it was an ideal way to enjoy meals.

In those days, many Americans consumed a lot of fast food every day. It seemed to Waters that no one cared about the ingredients they ate or how to cook them for their meals. Waters was *saddened because cheap and unhealthy fast food was shaping people's eating habits and had become deeply embedded in American food culture. She believed people should make more conscious choices about ③what to eat in their daily lives. While she was not a professional cook at the time, she soon began inviting her friends over to her house and cooking food for them using fresh ingredients. She found joy in serving food to others, and having her own restaurant where she could offer healthy and nutritious meals became her dream.

④Waters' dream came true in 1971 when she opened her own French restaurant, *Chez Panisse, in Berkeley. Overcoming the challenges *posed by the COVID-19 pandemic, the U.S.'s first *farm-to-table restaurant celebrated its 50th anniversary in August 2021.

(383 words)

注：Berkeley　バークレー（米国カリフォルニア州の都市）
　　　come together at ～　～に（大勢で）やって来る　　　pioneer　（新しいこと）を始める
　　　scattered across ～　～中に散らばった　　　sadden　～を悲しませる
　　　Chez Panisse　シェ・パニーズ（レストラン名）　　　pose　～をもたらす
　　　farm-to-table　地元産の食材を使った料理を出す（「農場からテーブルへ」が直訳）

(1)　下線部①の意味を具体的に説明している箇所を本文中から探し，ひと続きの英語 5 語で抜き出しなさい。

_____

(2)　下線部②に関して，フランス留学中のアリス・ウォータースに感銘を与えたのは人々のどのような生活でしたか。（　　　）を補い，日本文を完成させなさい。

　　人々が（　　　　　　　　　　　　　　　　　　　　　　　　　　　　）を家で調理し，家族といっしょに食べていたこと。

(3)　下線部③とほぼ同じ意味で用いられている英語 4 語を本文中から探して答えなさい。

_____

(4)　下線部④に関して，アリス・ウォータースの夢とはどのようなものでしたか。30 〜 35 字の日本語で説明しなさい。

_____

(5)　本文の内容と一致するものを 2 つ選び，記号で答えなさい。

　ア　The purpose of the Edible Schoolyard Project is to provide students with an opportunity to learn about food and the land it comes from.

　イ　Alice Waters has supported the Edible Schoolyard Project as the founder of Martin Luther King Jr. Middle School.

　ウ　Alice Waters, who stayed in France during her university years, loved the way people enjoyed local food.

　エ　Alice Waters believes fast food is essential for busy Americans to get regular meals every day.

　オ　It has been almost 50 years since Alice Waters opened Chez Panisse, a farm-to-table French restaurant, in Berkeley.

1   Choose the correct answer.

(1) My father is a (linguist / linguistics), and he studies many different languages.

(2) The Eiffel Tower in Paris is (renowned / renown) for its beauty and history.

(3) Lucy, as well as I, (wants / want) to join the art club.

2   Fill in the blanks to complete the sentences.

(1) 音楽のない世界で暮らすのはどんなでしょうか。

I wonder (   ) it (   ) be (   ) to live in the world without music.

(2) その地区にはこの数年で急にたくさんの店ができました。

New shops have (   ) (   ) in the district over the past few years.

(3) その画家はわずか数点しか絵画を描きませんでしたが，彼はそれらによって国際的な評価を得ています。

The artist created only a few paintings, (   ) (   ) he has gained an international reputation.

(4) 甘いお菓子を一度にたくさん食べ過ぎるとお腹が痛くなるかもしれません。

Eating too much candy at one time can (   ) (   ) a stomachache.

3   Reorder the words in brackets so that they make sense.

(1) (allowed / outside / you'll / to / be / play) after finishing your homework.

_____

(2) The sick man (isolated / was / the other passengers / from / being) on the ship.

_____

(3) My parents (a lie / telling / condemned / for / me).

_____

4   Translate the Japanese into English.

(1) 突然雨が降り出すまでは，すべてがうまくいっていました。(go を使って)

_____

(2) 生徒のだれもその質問に対する答えがわかりませんでした。

_____

(3) インターネットのおかげで，その歌は一夜にして人気になりました。

_____

(4) 子どもたちは社会の規則を守るように教えられるべきです。

_____

1　Choose the correct answer.

(1)　Parrots are good at (mimicing / mimicking) human speech and sounds.

(2)　Sharks have many sharp (teeth / tooth) in their mouths.

(3)　We use our (lung / lungs) to breathe in fresh air.

2　Fill in the blanks to complete the sentences.

(1)　"cat" という単語は，2つの子音の間に1つの母音を含んでいます。

　　The word "cat" contains one (　　　　　) sound between two (　　　　　) sounds.

(2)　その2つの生物種を区別する大きな特徴とは何ですか。

　　What are the major (　　　　　) (　　　　　) those two species?

(3)　キャリアにおいて一歩先にスタートを切っておけば，非常に有利になるでしょう。

　　If you have a (　　　　　) (　　　　　) in your career, it will be a great advantage.

(4)　赤ん坊は生まれたときは言葉を話せないが，親とコミュニケーションを交わすために泣く。

　　Babies can't talk (　　　　　) (　　　　　), but they can cry to communicate with their parents.

(5)　言語はコミュニケーションにおける重要な要素です。

　　Language is an (　　　　　) (　　　　　) in communication.

3　Reorder the words in brackets so that they make sense.

(1)　(the lid / the jar / tighten / remember / to / on) so that it won't spill.

　　_____

(2)　Tom and Bill (to / about / have / a lot / common / talk / in).

　　_____

(3)　(if / all / disappeared / what / the rain forests) from Earth?

　　_____

4　Translate the Japanese into English.

(1)　そのチームは歴史的建造物の修復に関わっています。(involved を使って)

　　_____

(2)　騒音があまりにもひどかったので，彼は耳を指でふさぎました。

　　_____

(3)　この花瓶(the vase)をどこに置いたらよいかわかりません。

　　_____

(4)　私が買い物を終えて帰宅したころには，外はすでに暗くなっていました。(time を使って)

　　_____

1 Choose the correct answer.

(1) If you practice, you will (assuredly / assured) improve your soccer skills.

(2) The rain fell (continuously / continuous) throughout the day.

(3) The two countries took the (initial / initiative) step toward peace.

(4) When you swallow, the food goes down your (throat / cheeks).

2 Fill in the blanks to complete the sentences.

(1) 火のそばに寄って，体を温めなさい。

(   ) (   ) (   ) the fire and warm yourself.

(2) その国について私たちが得られる情報は極めて限られています。

The information we can get about the country is (   ) (   ).

(3) 今度は風景画を描いてみてはどうですか。

What (   ) (   ) to paint a landscape next time?

(4) メッセージが届くと，電話が振動するのがわかります。

You can feel a phone (   ) when a message arrives.

3 Reorder the words in brackets so that they make sense.

(1) This is (movie / watched / the / have / best / I / ever / very).

_____

(2) (able / you / not / distinguish / will / be / to) between the two pictures.

_____

(3) Some people can (what / lips / by / understand / being / is / said / reading).

_____

4 Translate the Japanese into English.

(1) 強いハリケーン(hurricane)がフロリダ州(the state of Florida)に近づいています。

_____

(2) たくさん練習すればするほど，あなたはピアノを弾くのが上手になるでしょう。

〈〈the＋比較級〉を使って〉

_____

(3) 先生は私の英語の手紙にあった文法上の(grammatical)誤りをいくつか直しました。

_____

(4) その本はあなたにタイタニック号(the Titanic)に起きたことを教えてくれるでしょう。

_____

Part 4　基本問題

1　Choose the correct answer.

(1)　Paul likes (mathematics / mathematic) the best of all the subjects.

(2)　Can you please (take away / take over) the empty plates from the table?

(3)　She can (interpret / interpreter) several languages.

2　Fill in the blanks to complete the sentences.

(1)　そのソフトウェアの更新ファイルがまもなく入手可能になります。

　　　The update for the software will (　　　　) (　　　　　) soon.

(2)　仕事で成功を収めたおかげで，ジャックは以前よりも暮らし向きがよくなっています。

　　　Thanks to his successful career, Jack is (　　　　) (　　　　　) than he used to be.

(3)　ローマ帝国の最盛期には，その文化は広範囲に伝播（でんぱ）しました。

　　　(　　　　) the (　　　　　) of the Roman Empire, their culture spread far and wide.

(4)　オペラのことになると，ポールは話が止まらなくなります。

　　　(　　　) (　　　　) (　　　　　) to opera, Paul can't stop talking about it.

(5)　親は子どもたちにいっそう多くの読み書きの能力を高める機会を与えるべきです。

　　　Parents should offer their children more opportunities to promote (　　　　　).

3　Reorder the words in brackets so that they make sense.

(1)　Bill (happened / tends / what / exaggerate / him / to / to).

　　　_____

(2)　You'll (better / studying / be / the test / for / off) instead of watching TV.

　　　_____

(3)　(skill level / is / the team / average / of / the) improving steadily.

　　　_____

4　Translate the Japanese into English.

(1)　その病気は主に熱帯地方で流行しています。

　　　_____

(2)　その大会で彼が優勝したのは当然です。（surprise を使って）

　　　_____

(3)　デザートにはケーキかアイスクリームのどちらかが選べます。

　　　_____

(4)　買い物に行く途中，私は空に虹を見ました。（on を使って）

　　　_____

TV Captions

Today, most of the TV programs produced in Japan are broadcast with ①captions — sentences or groups of words that explain what is currently being shown. Viewers can access this text information during broadcasting by switching to the "captioned" mode. The main purpose of captions is to assist individuals who are deaf or hard of hearing in

5　understanding the content of TV programs.

Essentially, TV captions *transcribe the audio *portion of a program as it occurs, and they often include descriptions of non-speech elements. Particularly in dramas, non-speech elements such as sound effects, music, the manner of speaking, and speaker identification, are crucial for understanding the events on the screen. By reading these

10　captions, deaf and hard-of-hearing individuals can enjoy TV program content and access information without relying on *additional devices.

The history of TV captions began when *Julia Child, an American chef, taught viewers a chicken recipe on *The French Chef*, *WGBH's cooking program, on August 5, 1972. During the cooking program, TV captions were used so that deaf and hard-of-

15　hearing Americans could enjoy the audio portion of a national television program. ② It was a truly epoch-making experiment, and it opened the world of television to individuals who are deaf and hard of hearing. In fact, after *The French Chef*, captioned programs became a new standard for television experiences.

One significant issue with ③the early captioned TV programs was that viewers had

20　to watch the captions all the time on the TV screen, ④whether they needed to or not. This method, called open captioning, did not give viewers the option to turn off the text displayed on the screen. This problem persisted until 1980, when closed captioning technology was finally *put into practice on some TV programs in the U.S.

Since then, captioning technology has significantly improved. Captions have become

25　much more accurate and *precise, and they are *universally available on any television. Now, not only TV broadcast services but also streaming services on the Internet provide captioning options, (　⑤　) deaf or hard-of-hearing individuals to access the information they need. Captions have become a *necessity for promoting a barrier-free society.

(353 words)

注：transcribe　〜を文字に起こす　　portion　部分　　additional　追加の，さらなる
　　Julia Child　ジュリア・チャイルド（アメリカの女性シェフ・作家）

38

WGBH　ボストンの国内向け教育テレビ局(現在は公共放送局)
put ～ into practice　～を実用化する　　precise　正確な
universally　広く, 一般に　　necessity　必要不可欠なもの

(1)　下線部①は, 何を目的とするものか。(　　　)を補い, 日本文を完成させなさい。
　　(

　　　　　　　　　　　　　　　　　　　　　　　　　　　　　　　　　　　)ため。

(2)　下線部②に関して, Julia Child の料理番組の放送のどこが「画期的な試み」だったのか。日本語で説明しなさい。
　　_____

(3)　下線部③に関して, 初期の字幕放送システムで視聴者ができなかったことは何か。本文中のひと続きの英語8語を抜き出して答えなさい。
　　_____

(4)　下線部④の to のあとに省略されている英語3語を補いなさい。
　　　　　_____　_____　_____

(5)　⑤に入る語として正しいものを1つ選び, 記号で答えなさい。
　　ア　begging　　イ　enabling　　ウ　ordering　　エ　warning
　　　　　　　　　　　　　　　　　　　　　　　　　　　　　　(　　　)

(6)　本文の内容と一致するものを2つ選び, 記号で答えなさい。
　　ア　Non-speech elements are often described in the TV captions because they are essential for understanding what is happening on the screen.
　　イ　The early captioning system required people to purchase optional devices when they wanted to use it.
　　ウ　*The French Chef* became popular among TV viewers in the U.S. after it introduced a closed captioning system.
　　エ　The invention of the closed captioning system became a turning point in realizing barrier-free television experiences.
　　オ　It was not until 1980 that closed captioning technology was put into practice on TV programs.

1 Choose the correct answer.

(1) Some plants have (resistance / resistant) to insects, so they don't get eaten.

(2) Our bodies are made up of many tiny (cellular / cellar) parts.

(3) Grandma sometimes forgets things because she has (dementia / inflammation).

(4) Our brains have (plasticity / plasticize), so they can learn new things easily.

2 Fill in the blanks to complete the sentences.

(1) 政府は景気のてこ入れを続けています。

The government is continuing to (   ) (   ) the economy.

(2) 他の人々に親切にすれば，今度は彼らがあなたに親切にしてくれるかもしれません。

If you're kind to others, they might be kind to you (   ) (   ).

(3) 残念なことにアリスが行くとアイスクリーム店は閉まっていました。

(   ) her (   ), Alice found the ice cream shop closed.

(4) その自動車工場の閉鎖によって，市の経済にはかなりの影響が及ぶでしょう。

The closing of the automobile factory will have considerable (   ) for the city's economy.

3 Reorder the words in brackets so that they make sense.

(1) (us / it / impossible / reverse / for / to / is) the course of history.

_____

(2) (of / the amount / important / plastic waste / is / reducing) for the environment.

_____

(3) (the actor / eludes / the name / me / just / of) at the moment.

_____

4 Translate the Japanese into English.

(1) その図書館には私たちが読むべき興味深い本がたくさんあります。(wealth を使って)

_____

(2) その消防士(firefighter)ははしごを使って木の上からネコを助け出しました。

_____

(3) 放置されれば，ネズミの個体数(population)は急速に増えることでしょう。

_____

(4) 健康的な食べ物を食べれば，あなたは体力がつくでしょう。

_____

1　Choose the correct answer.

(1)　Water is made up of tiny (molecular / cognitive) parts.

(2)　Emma and I are (collaborators / collaborations) on our science project.

(3)　The (linkage / relation) between the two gears makes the machine work.

(4)　Our glasses help correct our vision (impairment / impair).

(5)　He always helps his friends without (rewards / awards).

2　Fill in the blanks to complete the sentences.

(1)　何か重いものを持ち上げるためには筋肉を使います。

　　You use your (　　　　　　) to lift something heavy.

(2)　ケンは健康を維持するために毎朝公園をジョギングします。

　　Ken jogs in the park every morning in (　　　　　) (　　　　　) stay healthy.

(3)　その登山家は正午前に山の頂上に着きました。

　　The climber (　　　　) the (　　　　　) of the mountain before noon.

(4)　糖分の取り過ぎはしばしば肥満のリスクを高めることと関連づけられます。

　　Eating too much sugar is often (　　　　　) (　　　　　) an increased risk of obesity.

(5)　研究者たちはその新薬のネズミに対する効果を検証中です。

　　The researchers are (　　　　) the (　　　　　) of the new medicine on mice.

3　Reorder the words in brackets so that they make sense.

(1)　The doctor (a vaccine / injected / with / the patient's arm).

　　_____

(2)　Math and physics (other / are / to / related / each).

　　_____

(3)　The smell of baking cookies (to / induced / come / everyone) into the kitchen.

　　_____

4　Translate the Japanese into English.

(1)　そのトンネルがいつ復旧する (be reopened) かはまだはっきりしません。

　　_____

(2)　その植物種は熱帯地方にだけ存在する (exist) ことが知られています。

　　_____

(3)　宇宙がどのようにして生まれたかについてわかっていることは，はるかに少ないのです。

　　　　　　　　　　　　　　　　　　　　　　　　　　　　　　　(create を使って)

　　_____

1 Choose the correct answer.

(1) He examined the tiny organisms (microscopically / microscopic).

(2) The snow on the mountaintop looked (untouched / unchecked) and pure.

(3) The driver was not satisfied with the (output / outcome) of the race.

(4) As we climb higher, the air gets (progressively / willingly) colder.

2 Fill in the blanks to complete the sentences.

(1) 彼は靴ひもがほどけたので締め直しました。

His shoelaces (   ) (   ), so he tied them again.

(2) サラは自分で焼いたアーモンドクッキーを 1 枚 1 枚別々に包みました。

Sarah (   ) (   ) the almond cookies she baked.

(3) 科学者はその細胞の大きさを正確に計りました。

The scientist measured the size of the tissue with (   ).

(4) キャロルはキッチンで朝食を作っていました。その間，夫は犬を散歩させていました。

Carol was cooking breakfast in the kitchen. (   ), her husband was walking his

dog.

(5) クラスの半数の生徒は数学が好きですが，もう半数の生徒は科学のほうが好きです。

Half of the class like math, (   ) the other half prefer science.

3 Reorder the words in brackets so that they make sense.

(1) Bill had to study hard to (the level / catch / math / to / of / up) taught in his class.

_____

(2) The symptoms of COVID-19 (the flu / are / those / similar / of / to).

_____

(3) You (your umbrella / have / the bus / left / on / might).

_____

4 Translate the Japanese into English.

(1) 物事を違う観点から見ているので，私たちの意見は異なるのです。

_____

(2) ダム建設工事は予定よりもはるかに遅れています。(lag を使って)

_____

(3) 私たちが着くまでに美術館はすでに閉まっていました。

_____

(4) 日が沈む(go down)とともに辺りは暗くなりました。

_____

1　Choose the correct answer.

(1)　He (rarely / barely) eats candy because he knows it's not healthy.

(2)　(Enzymes / Neurons) help our bodies break down food.

(3)　We want to (remake / remodel) our kitchen so that it looks new and fresh.

(4)　The mosquito bite might (inflame / inflammation) your skin.

2　Fill in the blanks to complete the sentences.

(1)　電球を省エネの LED に交換することを検討したほうがいいでしょう。

　　You should (　　　　　　) (　　　　　　　　) replacing the bulb with an energy-saving LED.

(2)　その箱には子供が遊ぶおもちゃがいっぱい入っていました。

　　The box was (　　　　　　) (　　　　　　　) toys for the children to play with.

(3)　健康的な朝食を食べれば 1 日を元気に始めることができます。

　　Eating a healthy breakfast can (　　　　　　　) your day with energy.

(4)　マイクは彼の父親と外見が本当によく似ています。

　　Mike really (　　　　　) his father in (　　　　　　　).

(5)　その薬の開発は事実上中止されました。

　　The development of the medicine was, (　　　　　　) (　　　　　　　), canceled.

3　Reorder the words in brackets so that they make sense.

(1)　The evidence found at the fire scene (suggestive / a gas leak / is / of).

　　_____

(2)　Make sure (your seatbelt / you / strap / on) before the car starts moving.

　　_____

4　Translate the Japanese into English.

(1)　天気予報を見れば，明日雨が降るかどうかわかるでしょう。(tell を使って)

　　_____

(2)　その装置は身体上の障害を抱えた人たちにとって助けとなるでしょう。(those を使って)

　　_____

(3)　夏の暑い日にアイスクリームを食べるのが好きではない人なんていません。

　　　　　　　　　　　　　　　　　　　　　　　　　　　(Who で始めて)

　　_____

(4)　バスの大部分は後部にエンジンがあります。(rear を使って)

　　_____

Does Exercise *Boost Your Memory?

In today's *health-conscious world, more and more people are realizing the importance of engaging in regular physical activity. Some people never miss jogging to kick-start their day. Others spend considerable amounts of money going to a gym to *work out after work. In fact, moderate or *vigorous exercise has ①many health benefits.
5　It maintains your muscle strength, strengthens your *immune system to fight against diseases, and helps control your body weight. However, have you ever wondered how short bursts of physical activity can boost your memory and thinking skills?

In a recent study published in the *Journal of Epidemiology & Community Health in January 2023, researchers tracked data from nearly 4,500 people in the U.K. who
10　wore activity monitors for 24 hours a day for a week straight. ②Based on the data, they *analyzed how their activity levels impacted their short-term memory, problem-solving skills, and ability to process things. The researchers found that doing moderate or vigorous exercise and activities was linked to significantly higher ③cognitive scores — the scores that show how well your brain is functioning — than people who spent most
15　of their time sitting, sleeping, or doing gentle activities. Vigorous exercise generally includes activities such as running, swimming, and cycling *uphill. On the other hand, moderate exercise includes walking at a faster pace than usual and any activity that accelerates your heart rate.

One of the most remarkable findings was that people who did workouts for a specific
20　period of time showed better *working memory. They also showed better performance in executive processes, which are higher-level cognitive functions that require *complex thinking, problem-solving, and decision-making, such as planning tasks, managing time effectively, and making strategic choices.

The researchers say that even engaging in physical activities for less than 10 minutes
25　can enhance your cognitive levels. Further research is needed to understand the long-term effects of exercise on cognitive health. However, even if you don't enjoy being physically active, dedicating even a short amount of time to regular exercise every day could be a good idea. Beginning ④this habit today could enable you to continue enjoying cognitive health for the rest of your life. Why not take that step today?

(368 words)

注：boost　〜を促進する　　health-conscious　健康志向の

work out　運動して汗を流す　　vigorous　激しい

immune system　免疫システム

Journal of Epidemiology & Community Health

　　医学雑誌名（＊ epidemiology は「疫学」の意）

analyze　〜を分析する　　uphill　上り坂で

working memory

　　作業記憶（情報を一時的に保持しながら，必要な操作や判断を同時に処理する能力）

complex　複雑な

(1)　下線部①の具体例のうち，「記憶力」や「思考力」に関連する以外のものを日本語で3つ答えなさい。

　　・＿＿＿＿＿＿＿＿＿＿＿＿＿＿＿＿＿＿＿＿＿＿＿＿＿＿＿＿＿＿＿＿＿＿＿＿＿＿

　　・＿＿＿＿＿＿＿＿＿＿＿＿＿＿＿＿＿＿＿＿＿＿＿＿＿＿＿＿＿＿＿＿＿＿＿＿＿＿

　　・＿＿＿＿＿＿＿＿＿＿＿＿＿＿＿＿＿＿＿＿＿＿＿＿＿＿＿＿＿＿＿＿＿＿＿＿＿＿

(2)　下線部②に関して，研究者たちはどのようなことを発見したのか。（　　　　）を補い，日本文を完成させなさい。

　　一定期間（　　　　　　　　　　　　　　　　　　　　　　　　　）により，

　　（　　　　　　　　　　　　　　　　　　　　　　　　　）が大幅に高くなった。

(3)　下線部③は何を測定するためのものか。本文中のひと続きの英語6語で答えなさい。

　　＿＿＿＿＿＿＿＿＿＿＿＿＿＿＿＿＿＿＿＿＿＿＿＿＿＿＿＿＿＿＿＿＿＿＿＿＿＿＿

(4)　下線部④はどのような習慣か。日本語で具体的に説明しなさい。

　　＿＿＿＿＿＿＿＿＿＿＿＿＿＿＿＿＿＿＿＿＿＿＿＿＿＿＿＿＿＿＿＿＿＿習慣。

(5)　本文の内容と一致するものを2つ選び，記号で答えなさい。

　ア　Even though many people engage in regular physical activity, few of them are aware of its health benefits.

　イ　Researchers found that both moderate and vigorous exercise were linked to higher cognitive performance.

　ウ　The researchers analyzed the data gathered from more than 4,000 participants for a long period of time.

　エ　The longer people engaged in physical activity, the better performance they showed in executive processes.

　オ　It is still not clear how engaging in regular physical activity can affect cognitive health on a long-term basis.

1 Choose the correct answer.

(1) A (flock / herd) of cows grazed in the field.

(2) She had an (inclined / inclination) to love drawings and paintings.

(3) We got lost because the map was (accurate / inaccurate).

(4) We have to get her teacher's (approval / approve) before starting our project.

2 Fill in the blanks to complete the sentences.

(1) 彼は人生における大きな課題に直面していました。

He was (　　　　　) (　　　　　　　) a big challenge in his life.

(2) チームメンバーたちは試合に勝つために協力しました。

The team members (　　　　　) (　　　　　　) together to win games.

(3) ミカは新しいクラスメイトたちとすぐに仲良しになれました。

Mika was able to (　　　　　) (　　　　　　) her new classmates quickly.

(4) ポーラはそのダイヤモンドが本物だと露ほども疑わずに信じています。

Paula believes, (　　　　　) a (　　　　　) of a (　　　　　　), that the diamond is genuine.

(5) その2人は楽園から追放されました。

The two were (　　　　　) (　　　　　　) of paradise.

(6) その2つの部族は領地をめぐって対立しました。

Those two tribes (　　　　　) (　　　　　) (　　　　　　) over territory.

3 Reorder the words in brackets so that they make sense.

(1) She carefully (was / before / considered / her / laid / what) before making a decision.

_____

(2) (seemed / last / the meeting / to) forever.

_____

(3) The mystery (made / has / clear / been / not) yet.

_____

4 Translate the Japanese into English.

(1) マサオは友人たちを説得していっしょにパーティーに行きました。

_____

(2) 私たちは彼女を説得しようとしましたが，彼女は考えを変えようとしませんでした。

_____

(3) 私たちが得た情報は誤りとわかりました。

_____

1 Choose the correct answer.

(1) The two countries decided to become (allies / ally) and help each other.

(2) The ancient philosopher had many (disciples / disciplines) who followed his teachings.

(3) She had a (pragmatic / pragmatism) approach to solving the problem.

(4) Parents should serve as a child's (protector / protect).

2 Fill in the blanks to complete the sentences.

(1) 正直は最良の策であるというのが彼の信念です。

His (   ) is that honesty is the best policy.

(2) ほとんどの犬は家にいるよりも外で遊ぶほうが好きです。

Most dogs prefer playing outside (   ) (   ) staying home.

(3) ケヴィンは外見はあまり気にしません。

Kevin does not much (   ) (   ) he looks.

(4) ほかにいいアイディアが浮かばなかったので，彼はパーティーの余興に歌を歌いました。

(   ) (   ) of a better idea, he sang a song as entertainment at the party.

(5) この世界は今後何年にもわたって未曾有の異常気象を経験する可能性が非常に高い。

The world is (   ) (   ) to experience unprecedented extreme weather

for many years to come.

3 Reorder the words in brackets so that they make sense.

(1) Karen (a lot / her friends / about / cares).

_____

(2) The survey (a better way / revealed / the issue / handle / to).

_____

(3) (choose / to / the two / when / between / having), many people select the easier one.

_____

4 Translate the Japanese into English.

(1) ((店頭で))その赤いスカーフをすれば，あなたはもっと魅力的に見えるでしょう。

_____

(2) 私の祖母はそのネコを喜んで引き取りました。

_____

(3) 英語の本を読むことはあなたの語彙力(vocabulary)をアップするのに役立ちます。

_____

1 Choose the correct answer.

(1) She often spends time on social media to avoid the feeling of (lonely / loneliness).

(2) The bird's colorful feathers are its (distinctive / distinguish) feature.

(3) The audience was amazed by his (comparable / incomparable) musical talent.

(4) Different cultures have different (worldviews / worldviewings).

2 Fill in the blanks to complete the sentences.

(1) 私たちはアランに夢を(捨てずに)追求し続けるように説得しました。

We (　　　　　) Alan (　　　　　　　) continue pursuing his dream.

(2) 財産を失うリスクは犯す人はだれもいないでしょう。

No one will (　　　　　) the (　　　　　　　) of losing their fortune.

(3) 一生懸命に働けば報われるという信念は成功を収めるのに大切です。

The (　　　　　) (　　　　　　　) hard work pays off is important for success.

(4) その戦争によって多くの家族が引き裂かれました。

Many families were (　　　　　) (　　　　　　　) by the war.

(5) サルの赤ちゃんは母親の背中にしがみついていました。

The baby monkey was (　　　　　) (　　　　　　　) its mother's back.

3 Reorder the words in brackets so that they make sense.

(1) Some groups (integrated / dislike / society / into / being) due to various reasons.

_____

(2) (proximity / people / in / the park / living / close / to) can enjoy its benefits.

_____

(3) It (suspicious / made / the reliability / about / me) of the news.

_____

4 Translate the Japanese into English.

(1) 彼女はそのすぐれた仕事によって称賛(praise)を受けて当然です。

_____

(2) 今時スマートフォンを持っていないというのは奇妙に思われるかもしれません。

_____

(3) 2人のランナーがほぼ同時にゴールインしました。(reach the finish line を使って)

_____

(4) その点に関して私はあなたの意見に反対です。

_____

48

1　Choose the correct answer.

(1)　Close your eyes and (visualize / visual) your favorite place.

(2)　His idea is radical, but it deserves (consideration / considerate).

(3)　The boys tried to pull the rope (to / in) their direction.

(4)　The artist had an (eccentric / essential) style and painted unique pictures.

2　Fill in the blanks to complete the sentences.

(1)　この車はその価値を高めるような特徴をいくつか備えています。

This vehicle has several features that (　　　　　) it (　　　　　).

(2)　意見の相違のために友人同士の間で口論が起きることはあり得ます。

Arguments can (　　　　　) (　　　　　) friends when they have different opinions.

(3)　ダムは渓谷の一方の側からもう一方の側にまたがっています。

The dam stretches from (　　　　) side to (　　　　) (　　　　) of the valley.

(4)　その橋の両端には国境検問所があります。

Border checkpoints are located on (　　　　) (　　　　) of the bridge.

(5)　絵を描くことに関しては，彼女はクラスでいちばんです。

When (　　　　) (　　　　) to painting pictures, she's the best in our class.

3　Reorder the words in brackets so that they make sense.

(1)　The money (spent / would / saving / better / on / be) the victims of the typhoon.

_____

(2)　My boss (my idea / difficult / too / dismissed / as).

_____

4　Translate the Japanese into English.

(1)　自分では変えられないことをくよくよ悩んでもむだです。(sense を使って)

_____

(2)　そのイヌは，ボールを追いかけながら，公園の中をすごい勢いで(wildly)走っていました。

_____

(3)　私たちはグループ・プロジェクトを完成させるために一丸となって働きました。

(unit を使って)

_____

(4)　そのケーキを8つに分けましょう。(divide を使って)

_____

*Exploring the Meanings of 'Mind'

After studying English for many years, you might have discovered one thing: ①as a word becomes more basic, it tends to have more meanings and usages. Many basic English words have their roots in *Old English, and they have gained *numerous meanings and usages through their *evolution over time. Is 'mind' one of ②these challenging basic words for English learners? If you look up the word in your dictionary, you'll be surprised at the range and depth of its meanings.

First of all, 'mind' is commonly used to refer to the way a person thinks, feels, and uses their *intellect, often in *idiomatic expressions. For instance, you can say, "She has finally made up her mind to study abroad." You can also convince someone to 'change their mind.' Also, a well-known proverb goes, "So many men, so many minds." It means "⎡   ③   ⎤, so it is natural they think and behave differently." In these cases, 'mind' can be translated as 'kangae (考え)' or 'kangae-kata (考え方)' in Japanese.

Moving on to another important usage, 'mind' is used to refer to a person's *mentality. For example, when you say, "I'm losing my mind trying to finish this job on time," it indicates your mental condition is very (④   ) because of the stress from working too hard. Furthermore, the *idiom 'out of *one's* mind' refers to a negative mental condition, as seen in a sentence like "You must be out of your mind to swim in the sea on such a cold day." It means '(⑤   ).' The noun 'mind' used in these examples means 'kokoro (心)' or 'ki (気)' in Japanese.

Additionally, the word 'mind' is used as a verb in many *ordinary situations. ⑥"Never mind." is introduced into the Japanese language in an incorrect way as 'don-mai (ドンマイ),' one of the typical *Japanese English phrases. "Mind your own business." is used as a warning, meaning "⎡   ⑦   ⎤" When you ask someone to take a picture of you and your friend, you can say, "Would you mind taking our picture?"

What has been discussed above represents only a small part of the meanings and usages associated with the word 'mind'. How about exploring the word further for yourself by looking it up in a dictionary and discovering additional interesting examples?

(386 words)

注：explore 　〜を調べる，探求する　　Old English　古英語(700 〜 1150 年頃の英語)
numerous　非常に多くの　　evolution　展開，変化　　intellect　知性，知力
idiomatic expression　慣用表現　　mentality　心理，精神状態
idiom　イディオム，慣用句　　ordinary　日常的な
Japanese English phrase　　和製英語

(1)　下線部①とほぼ同じ内容を表すように，次の英文の＿＿に適切な英語を書きなさい。
　　　＿＿＿＿＿＿＿＿＿＿＿＿＿＿＿＿＿＿＿＿＿, the more meanings and usages it tends to have.

(2)　下線部②はどのような単語のことか。35 字程度の日本語で説明しなさい。
　　　＿＿＿＿＿＿＿＿＿＿＿＿＿＿＿＿＿＿＿＿＿＿＿＿＿＿＿＿＿＿＿＿＿＿＿＿＿＿＿

(3)　③，⑦の□□に入る文として正しいものをそれぞれ 1 つ選び，記号で答えなさい。
　　③　ア　We should share the same worldview
　　　　イ　Everyone has good points and bad points
　　　　ウ　Each person has unique ideas and tastes
　　　　エ　Having no worries is just a fantasy　　　　　　　　　　　　　　（　　　）
　　⑦　ア　Stop asking about my private affairs.
　　　　イ　Put in more effort and concentrate harder on your work.
　　　　ウ　Be kind to others for your own benefit.
　　　　エ　Be polite when you ask someone a favor.　　　　　　　　　　　（　　　）

(4)　④に入る適切な形容詞 1 語を書きなさい。ただし，b で始まる語とします。
　　　　　　　　　　　　　　　　　　　　　　　　　　　　　＿＿＿＿＿＿＿＿＿＿＿＿

(5)　⑤に入る語として正しいものを 1 つ選び，記号で答えなさい。
　　ア　comfortable　　イ　crazy　　ウ　exciting　　エ　solitary
　　　　　　　　　　　　　　　　　　　　　　　　　　　　　　　　　　　（　　　）

(6)　下線部⑥は何の例として使われているか。（　　　　）を補い，日本文を完成させなさい。
　　英語から日本語に（　　　　　　　　　　　　　　　　　　　　　）結果，
　　（　　　　　　　　　　　　　　　　　　　　　　　　　　　）表現の例。

1   Choose the correct answer.

(1)   From the evidence, we can (include / conclude) that the bear killed the cow.

(2)   The church is an important place for (theologically / theological) discussions.

(3)   The river was so wide that it seemed (uncrossable / unclimbable) without a bridge.

(4)   Grandpa likes to have (philosopher / philosophical) discussions about life.

(5)   The smell of grilling meat started to (permeate / traverse) the whole house.

2   Fill in the blanks to complete the sentences.

(1)   太陽は私たちに光と暖かさを提供するうえで中心的な役割を果たしています。

The sun (　　　　　) a central (　　　　　　) in giving us light and warmth.

(2)   計画が頓挫したあとで，彼らは事態を収拾しようと努めました。

After the project failed, they tried hard to (　　　　　) (　　　　　) the (　　　　　).

(3)   絵を描くための想像力を働かせる方法はいくらでもあります。

You can use your imagination to draw in (　　　　) (　　　　　) ways.

(4)   悪魔のことを話していると，きっと現れる。(((ことわざ))「うわさをすれば影」)

(　　　　) (　　　　　) the devil, and he is sure to appear.

(5)   先生はその数学の問題の解き方を説明しました。

The teacher (　　　　　) an (　　　　　　) of how to solve the math problem.

3   Reorder the words in brackets so that they make sense.

(1)   The heat in the desert (enough / without / can / unbearable / be / water).

_____

(2)   (you / the bird / what / call / do) in English?

_____

(3)   We must agree that (woman / a / she / most / is / talented).

_____

4   Translate the Japanese into English.

(1)   ジョンはバスの中で彼に話しかけてきた少女と恋に落ちました。

_____

(2)   よく晴れた夜の空には数え切れないほど多くの星が見えます。

_____

(3)   運動選手はより強くなるために多くのトレーニングに耐えなければなりません。

_____

1 Choose the correct answer.

(1) Sharing is an important value for (humankind / humankinds) to live together peacefully.

(2) Emily talked to a (therapy / therapist) to help her feel better when she was sad.

(3) Losing a pet can be a (devastating / devastated) experience for anyone.

(4) Lily nodded to (affirm / confirm) that she understood what her friend was saying.

(5) Dogs often show (affection / isolation) by wagging their tails at their owners.

2 Fill in the blanks to complete the sentences.

(1) その問題は本書の範囲を超えています。

The issue is (　　　　) the (　　　　) of this book.

(2) 少なくとも人材がもっと必要だという点では私たちは意見が一致しています。

We can (　　　　) (　　　　) agree that we need more human resources.

(3) 彼らの報酬アップの要求はかなえられました。

Their (　　　　) for a higher salary have been (　　　　).

(4) 良識のある人なら，そんな無責任な物言いはしないでしょうに。

A person with common sense (　　　　) (　　　　) make such (　　　　) remarks.

(5) 次の試合に勝ちたいなら，あなたはもっとトレーニングに励まなければなりません。

If you (　　　　) (　　　　) win the next game, you must train harder.

3 Reorder the words in brackets so that they make sense.

(1) (the heart / at / any culture / of / is) its language.

_____

(2) (be / seems / his desire / succeed / stronger / to / to) than others.

_____

(3) (more / is / playing / nothing / fun / games / than) with friends.

_____

4 Translate the Japanese into English.

(1) 栄養のある食べ物を毎日食べることは私たちの健康にとって欠かせません。

_____

(2) 多くの親たちは子どもをおもちゃやゲームで甘やかします。(indulge を使って)

_____

(3) そういうわけで私は短距離を移動するときはたいていバスを利用します。(why を使って)

_____

53

1 Choose the correct answer.

(1) Young children sometimes act in an (egocentrism / egocentric) way.

(2) Doctors and scientists work together to try to (eradicate / radicate) the disease.

(3) Winning the race filled Maria with a feeling of (euphoria / euphoric).

(4) It's (insincere / unrealistic) of you to expect to become an expert overnight.

(5) A unicorn is a (fancy / fanciful) creature that has a horn on its head.

2 Fill in the blanks to complete the sentences.

(1) 両チームとも試合中の天候の急変を考慮していませんでした。

Neither of the teams had (　　　　　) (　　　　　　　) sudden weather changes during the game.

(2) その赤いボールはティムのものです。彼がそれで遊ぶために持ってきたのです。

The red ball (　　　　　) (　　　　　　　) Tim; he brought it to play with.

(3) あなたは戦争がない世界を想像できますか。

Can you (　　　　　) (　　　　　　　) a world where there are no wars?

(4) ルーシーはいつも喜んで友だちの宿題を手伝います。

Lucy is always (　　　　　) (　　　　　　　) help her friends with their homework.

(5) 試験中は設問に集中することが大切です。

During the test, it's important to keep your (　　　　　) (　　　　　　　) the questions.

3 Reorder the words in brackets so that they make sense.

(1) The newcomer (be / emerged / a power / with / to / reckoned / as).

_____

(2) Alice and Sarah (their favorite book / feel / way / toward / the same).

_____

(3) (give / the media / the false sense / may / us) that we've already overcome COVID-19.

_____

4 Translate the Japanese into English.

(1) 時間を効率的に使えば，1日に多くのことを済ませることができます。

_____

(2) 私たちは環境のためにリサイクルを促進すべきです。（benefit を使って）

_____

(3) 地球やほかの惑星は太陽の周りを回っています。（revolve を使って）

_____

1   Choose the correct answer.

(1)   Babies have an (instinct / instinctual) need for love and care from their parents.

(2)   Finishing a puzzle gave Lily a sense of (satisfaction / satisfied).

(3)   Reading books can (enrich / rich) your mind and help you learn new things.

(4)   The owner had to (expend / expand) a lot of money to refurbish his restaurant.

2   Fill in the blanks to complete the sentences.

(1)   そのイベントの成功の功績はマリアの手柄とされるべきです。

Maria should (   ) (   ) for the success of the event.

(2)   持続可能な社会の実現への取り組みとして，自動車メーカーは省エネの自動車を開発しています。

Auto makers are developing energy-saving cars, (   ) (   ) (   ) to create a sustainable society.

(3)   深宇宙で起きていることは私たちの理解を超えています。

What is occurring in deep space (   ) (   ) our understanding.

(4)   一般の風邪は自然治癒に任せるのがよい。

The common cold just needs to (   ) its (   ).

(5)   その山の頂上からの眺めは，ハイキングでそこまで登るだけの価値があります。

The view from the top of the mountain is (   ) (   ) all the way up.

3   Reorder the words in brackets so that they make sense.

(1)   Birds fly south (the influence / their natural instincts / of / under).

_____

(2)   Barbara, (you / let / the table / me / help / set) for dinner.

_____

4   Translate the Japanese into English.

(1)   サラは外出する代わりに家にいて本を読むほうを選びました。

_____

(2)   彼はそのスピーチコンテストで1位になったことを誇りに思っています。

_____

(3)   鳥には卵を安全に保つために巣(nests)を作る本能があります。

_____

(4)   メンバー全員がそろうまで会議は始められません。(are here を使って)

_____

Pursuing Something You Love

　　We can't help but talk about something we love.　Soccer fans may talk *enthusiastically about their favorite team and players or the most exciting game they have ever watched.　Pet owners may tell you how their cats or dogs join their family and ①(are / how / them / their pets / to / precious).

5　　　We also like to talk about what we call hobbies — specific activities we love — such as taking photos, birding, and gardening.　One common factor among these activities is that you can enjoy ②them in your own way, within your budget and time, whether indoors or outdoors.　You don't necessarily need expensive devices or gadgets, and these hobbies are still *accessible to everyone.　The deeper your passion for these activities,

10　the harder it becomes to ③cut back on expenses.

　　Moving on to another aspect, our love for something often takes the form of a personal habit.　For example, ④some people love taking notes on every occasion in their daily lives.　They always carry a pen and a notebook to write down ideas or things to remember.　In the digital age, ⑤some people try to record everything that happens

15　to them using diary or calendar apps on their smartphones or computers.　Some even tweet about their experiences.　Such behavior can be seen as a personal habit, but the fact is that they genuinely love the act of taking notes and keeping records.

　　If you have a love for specific activities, consider pursuing them positively.　By ⑥doing so, you can find numerous ways to enrich your daily life.　[ア]　For instance, if

20　you have a passion for cooking, sharing your original recipes on social media *platforms can be *fulfilling.　[イ]　Many people have chosen careers related to their passions.　[ウ] However, if you don't have anything in particular that interests you *to the point of *losing track of time, why not start searching for it today?　[エ]

(330 words)

25

注：enthusiastically　熱狂的に　　　accessible　入手［利用］可能である
　　social media platform
　　　ソーシャルメディアプラットフォーム（X, Facebook, Instagram など）
　　fulfilling　充足感が得られる　　　to the point of 〜　（程度・段階が）〜というところまで
　　lose track of 〜　〜を見失う，〜がわからなくなる

(1) 下線部①が意味の通る英文となるように，（　　　）内の語句を並べかえなさい。

_____

(2) 下線部②が指す内容を本文中のひと続きの英語４語でそのまま書きなさい。

_____

(3) 下線部③が表す意味として最も適切と思われるものを１つ選び，記号で答えなさい。
  ア　make the best use of money　　イ　increase the budget
  ウ　use less money　　　　　　　　エ　justify the usage of money
                                                              （　　　）

(4) 下線部④，⑤のような人々に共通することは何か。30字程度の日本語で説明しなさい。

_____

(5) 下線部⑥の具体的内容を日本語で説明しなさい。

_____

(6) 以下の英文を補うのに適切な位置を，文中の[ア]〜[エ]から選び，記号で答えなさい。
Moreover, pursuing your favorite activities might lead you to think about your future career.
                                                              （　　　）

1   Choose the correct answer.

(1) The car's (velocity / altitude) increased as it went down the hill.

(2) The (subtle / subtlety) of the colors in the sunset was really beautiful.

(3) Her ticket was still (valid / invalid), so she was able to enter the theme park.

(4) The (freshman / freshmen) students were excited about their first day of school.

2   Fill in the blanks to complete the sentences.

(1) 証拠もなしに人を非難するのはよくありません。

(   ) an (   ) without evidence is not good.

(2) 学校側の決定に対して多くの生徒は反対の声を上げました。

Many students (   ) an (   ) to the school's decision.

(3) 時間はかかりましたが，ジョージは何とかそのパズルを解くことができました。

It took a while, but George finally managed to (   ) (   ) the puzzle.

(4) そのネコは自力でドアを開けることはできません。

The cat is (   ) (   ) opening the door by itself.

(5) こぼれてしまったミルクのことを嘆いても仕方がない。(((ことわざ))「覆水盆に返らず」)

There is (   ) (   ) in crying over spilled milk.

3   Reorder the words in brackets so that they make sense.

(1) (how / a discussion / about / improve / to / there's) the educational environment.

_____

(2) She felt (her / the police officer / stupid / look / made) in front of other people.

_____

4   Translate the Japanese into English.

(1) エマはケーキの最後の一切れを食べたと言って私のことを責めました。

_____

(2) その教授はフェミニスト・グループから抗議の手紙を受け取りました。

_____

(3) 私たちは大雨のために家にいなければなりませんでした。

_____

(4) 一部の発電所では発電するのに核エネルギーを使います。

_____

(5) その宇宙飛行士は国際宇宙ステーション(the ISS)から地球がどんなふうに見えたかを詳しく話しました。

_____

1 Choose the correct answer.

(1) The teacher read an (except / excerpt) from the story to the class.

(2) The test results were (satisfactory / unsatisfactory), so she decided to study harder next time.

(3) These days, she has been busy with personal (affairs / affair).

(4) The singer didn't get the desired (respond / response) from the audience.

2 Fill in the blanks to complete the sentences.

(1) 彼女は箱から一握りのキャンディーをつかみました。

She grabbed a (　　　　　) (　　　　　　　) candies from the box.

(2) 彼女は前方の友人たちに追いつくために走らなければなりませんでした。

She had to run to (　　　　　) (　　　　　　) with her friends ahead.

(3) ユカはそのイベントの責任者です。

Yuka is (　　　　) (　　　　　) (　　　　　　) organizing the event.

(4) 彼女は時間を確認するために時計をちらっと見ました。

She (　　　　　) (　　　　　) the clock to see the time.

(5) 彼らは通行人にチラシを配っていました。

They were (　　　　　) (　　　　　　) handbills to the passersby.

3 Reorder the words in brackets so that they make sense.

(1) She (invited / was / speak / the conference / to / at) about environmental issues.

_____

(2) In (were / several / of / the bank / police cars / front).

_____

(3) They (a prize / awarded / winning / her / for) the art competition.

_____

4 Translate the Japanese into English.

(1) 私の家族はイヌを2匹飼っています。1匹は黒で，もう1匹は茶色です。

_____

(2) 私は抗議活動の参加者たちが門の近くに立っているのを見ました。

_____

(3) 多くの会社はパソコンを3年おきくらいに買い替えます。

_____

(4) 彼は論文（essay）をよりよくするためにレポートを修正しなければなりませんでした。

_____

1 Choose the correct answer.

(1) Don't worry about such (trivia / trivial) matters.

(2) The crowd began to (chat / chant) slogans during the protest.

(3) She worked hard to get a (Ph.D. / D.Ph.) in psychology.

(4) It's important to treat everyone (with / without) prejudice.

(5) Drinking hot tea is a good (remedy / solidarity) for a sore throat.

2 Fill in the blanks to complete the sentences.

(1) 日が沈んだらすぐにキャンプファイアを始めます。

(   ) (   ) (   ) the sun sets, we'll start a campfire.

(2) 彼女は冷蔵庫に買う物を思い出せるように付箋を貼りました。

She put a sticky note on her fridge to (   ) her (   ) the grocery list.

(3) 世界中の多くの人々が性差別に苦しんでいます。

Many people around the world (   ) (   ) discrimination due to their gender.

(4) 道の両側には古い建物が並んでいます。

Old buildings are lined up (   ) (   ) side of the road.

(5) 抗議運動の参加者たちは国会議事堂まで行進しながら進みました。

The protestors (   ) (   ) to the Diet Building.

3 Reorder the words in brackets so that they make sense.

(1) (made / the party / everyone / her presence / happier / feel / at).

_____

(2) She (that / explained / her friend / to) the movie was going to start at 7:00.

_____

(3) (call / is / what / love / you / that)?

_____

4 Translate the Japanese into English.

(1) カナの両親は彼女に絵を描くことに対する情熱を追求する (pursue) ように勧めました。

_____

(2) 私たちのプロジェクトのためのよいアイディアはありますか。(think of を使って)

_____

(3) 彼は彼のおじさんのパーティーへの招待を丁重に断りました。

_____

1　Choose the correct answer.

(1)　She felt guilty and decided to (confess / convince) her mistake to her teacher.

(2)　The World Cup finals came to a (dramatic / drastic) end.

(3)　A (protein / proton) is a tiny particle found in the nucleus of an atom.

(4)　The (transcript / transform) of his speech is available on the Internet.

2　Fill in the blanks to complete the sentences.

(1)　彼女は眠っている赤ちゃんをそっとベビーベッドの中に下ろしました。

She gently (　　　　　　) her sleeping baby (　　　　　　) in the crib.

(2)　この山の険しさは富士山にはとても及ばないように思われます。

This mountain doesn't seem (　　　　　　) (　　　　　　) as steep as Mt. Fuji.

(3)　カナダの自然は彼女が想像していたよりもずっとすばらしかったです。

Nature in Canada was (　　　　　　) (　　　　　　) wonderful than she had imagined.

(4)　あなたは自分が生きたいように生きればよいのです。

You can live (　　　　) (　　　　) you want.

(5)　多くの消費者は食の安全に不安を抱いています。

Many consumers are (　　　　　) (　　　　　) food safety.

3　Reorder the words in brackets so that they make sense.

(1)　That is a little (actually / I / what / different / said / from).

_____

(2)　(forget / your grandmother / don't / call / to) on her birthday.

_____

4　Translate the Japanese into English.

(1)　その知らせを聞いたとき，私たちは互いに顔を見合わせました。

_____

(2)　私は数年前その会議で講演をしたことを覚えています。

_____

(3)　彼はこれまでにディベートで負けたことはなかったと私に話しました。

_____

(4)　その件に関しては私には何も言うことがありません。

_____

(5)　最近私が読んだ本についてお話ししたいと思います。

_____

'Ladies and Gentlemen'

You may have heard announcements that begin with the phrase 'Ladies and gentlemen.' Historically, this expression has been widely used to speak to a group or an audience, whether it's all ladies, all gentlemen, or a mix of ①both. Interestingly, you can use this phrase even when you're talking to just one person, whether they're
5　a gentleman or a lady. People have understood and accepted this for a long time. However, things are changing, and the way we use language is shifting to promote *gender inclusiveness by eliminating gender bias and stereotypes, and preventing gender-based discrimination.

In October 2019, Air Canada, one of the major Canadian airlines, announced that
10　②their flight crew would no longer greet passengers as 'ladies and gentlemen.' Instead, the flight crew started using *gender-neutral greetings such as "Good morning, everybody." Air Canada stated that the change in their *onboard announcement policy *reflects their effort to eliminate *gender-specific terms. This language change was also adapted for agents working at airport *boarding gates. Many other airlines, such as
15　Lufthansa in Germany and JAL in Japan, have made similar changes to their onboard announcement policies.

This shift is not limited to the airline industry. ③Today, an increasing number of corporations and organizations are working to remove gender-specific ideas as much as possible. This movement is often referred to as 'promoting gender inclusiveness,'
20　and using gender-neutral language is considered a crucial step toward creating a world where everyone is accepted without exception.

From the *perspective of English learners, you may *feel unsure about replacing gender-specific words with gender-neutral ones. For example, using 'police officer' instead of 'policeman,' 'chair' or 'chairperson' instead of 'chairman' or 'chairwoman,'
25　'server' instead of 'waiter' or 'waitress.' These days, even terms like 'brothers and sisters' are often replaced with '*siblings.' In fact, even native English speakers sometimes struggle or become confused when using gender-neutral language. ④(gender-neutral language / can / what / is / change / considered) over time. The key point to remember is that the language we use every day is closely connected to
30　how we *perceive and treat people.　(344 words)

62

注：gender inclusiveness　男女の性別による区別［差別］をしないこと
　　　gender-neutral　（特に言葉が）男女の区別のない
　　　onboard announcement　機内アナウンス
　　　reflect　〜を反映する　　gender-specific　一方の性に特定した
　　　boarding gate　搭乗ゲート　　perspective　見方，視点
　　　feel unsure about 〜　〜に戸惑いを覚える　　sibling　（男女の別なしに）きょうだい
　　　perceive　〜を理解する

(1)　下線部①が指すものを本文中の語を使って3語で答えなさい。

_____

(2)　航空会社のエア・カナダが下線部②のような方針変更を行った目的は何か。（　　　　）を補い，日本文を完成させなさい。

　　（　　　　　　　　　　　）から（　　　　　　　　　　　　　　　　　　）を排除するため。

(3)　下線部③のような動きが目指している目標とは何か。30字程度の日本語で説明しなさい。

_____

(4)　下線部④が意味の通る英文となるように，（　　　）内の語句を並べかえなさい。

_____

(5)　本文の内容と合うように，以下の(ア)〜(オ)に入る適切な語を1語ずつ書きなさい。

（　ア　）words	（　イ　）words
policeman	（　ウ　）
chairman	chairperson ／（　エ　）
waiter ／ waitress	（　オ　）

(6)　本文の内容と一致するものを1つ選び，記号で答えなさい。

　ア　So far, the shift to use gender-neutral language has been seen only in the airline industry.

　イ　These days, the word 'siblings' is used as a gender-neutral word to include 'brothers and sisters.'

　ウ　Making any language completely free from all gender bias and stereotypes is impossible.

1 Choose the correct answer.

(1) The government has been trying to (revitalize / refurbish) minority languages.

(2) The number of smartphone users has been (steadily / steady) decreasing.

(3) Many different (dialects / tribes) are spoken across our country.

2 Fill in the blanks to complete the sentences.

(1) キング牧師は公民権運動の指導者として知られています。

Dr. King is known as the leader of the (　　　　) (　　　　) (　　　　).

(2) そのハイウェイ建設計画は森林を保護する運動へとつながりました。

The highway construction project (　　　　) to (　　　　) to protect the forests.

(3) 私たちの困難な作業は次第に実を結び始めました。

Our hard work gradually began to (　　　　) (　　　　).

(4) この数か月間でガソリン価格が上昇しています。

Gasoline prices have been (　　　　) the (　　　　) over the last several months.

(5) そのレストランはとても小さいので，一度に6人しか入れません。

The restaurant is so small that it holds (　　　　) (　　　　) than six people at one time.

(6) 社会的少数者の権利はどのように守られるべきでしょうか。

How should the rights of (　　　　) (　　　　) be protected?

3 Reorder the words in brackets so that they make sense.

(1) In that country, (an official language / made / was / English) during World War II.

_____

(2) (in / took / many / 5,000 people / part / as / as) the marathon.

_____

4 Translate the Japanese into English.

(1) 一部の国では使い捨ての(single-use)ポリ袋が禁止されています。

_____

(2) 水がなければどんな植物も生き延びることはできないでしょう。

_____

(3) アラスカは1867年にアメリカ合衆国の一部になりました。

_____

(4) 古い伝統がいったん失われてしまえば，それらを回復させるのはほぼ不可能でしょう。

_____

1 Choose the correct answer.

(1) The (chapter / charter) for our club explains how we behave as members.

(2) Some students may (oppose / opposition) wearing uniforms to school.

(3) The government needs to (ratify / compromise) new laws before they become official.

(4) The (eliminate / elimination) of harmful substances from the water is essential.

(5) The team showed great (unity / unite) by working together to win the game.

2 Fill in the blanks to complete the sentences.

(1) 憲法第九条は何と宣言していますか。

What does Article 9 of the (　　　　　) (　　　　　)?

(2) 市議会はその歴史的建造物を保存する議案を可決しました。

The (　　　　　) (　　　　　) passed the bill to preserve the historical building.

(3) 市長は地元経済を活性化するための計画をいくつか提案しました。

The mayor (　　　　　) several plans to (　　　　　) the local economy.

(4) 従業員はストライキを決行するところまで行きました。

The employees (　　　　　) (　　　　　) (　　　　　) as going out on a strike.

(5) 彼女は自分の仕事に加えて，地元の動物保護施設でボランティアとして働いています。

(　　　　　) (　　　　　) (　　　　　) her job, she works as a volunteer at the local animal shelter.

3 Reorder the words in brackets so that they make sense.

(1) (is / between / a strong connection / there) exercise and staying healthy.

_____

(2) Some students (be / speak / may / to / unwilling) in front of the whole class.

_____

(3) (the shop / it / wonder / is / attracts / that / no) few customers.

_____

4 Translate the Japanese into English.

(1) そうこうするうちに出発時間が迫っていました。

_____

(2) 新しい技術の出現は私たちがコミュニケーションをする方法を変えました。

_____

(3) 大雨のために関東地方の公共交通機関は大きく乱れました。

_____

1 Choose the correct answer.

(1) The fence was an (obstruct / obstacle) that the dog couldn't jump over.

(2) The (imposition / position) of a new tax is facing public criticism.

(3) She (unequivocally / unequivocal) said no to selling her farm.

(4) Estonia's Language (Inspector / Inspectorate) is often called the "Language Police."

(5) A king or queen is a (sovereign / sovereignty) ruler of a country.

2 Fill in the blanks to complete the sentences.

(1) きれいな水は私たちの健康の維持において重要な役割を果たします。

Clean water (   ) an important (   ) in keeping us healthy.

(2) トムはしばしば野菜を食べるのを嫌がります。

Tom is often (   ) (   ) eat vegetables.

(3) 彼の説明はただの言い訳にしか聞こえませんでした。

His explanation sounded like (   ) (   ) excuses.

(4) 例えばジョギングを例にとりましょう。朝のジョギングは1日を始めるのによい方法です。

(   ), for example, jogging. Jogging in the morning is a good way to start the day.

(5) 先生は授業でプリントを配ったあと，続けてそれらについて説明しました。

After distributing handouts in class, the teacher (   ) (   ) explain them.

3 Reorder the words in brackets so that they make sense.

(1) Parents tend to (their children / on / impose / their ideas).

_____

(2) Many people (as / regard / their pets / of / part) their family.

_____

(3) He didn't (a hint / want / even / part / of / influence / others / from) when making his decision.

_____

4 Translate the Japanese into English.

(1) インドは 1947 年に独立しました。

_____

(2) 毎年日本国内外から多くの観光客がその温泉を訪れます。

_____

(3) 見渡す限り，空には雲一つありませんでした。

_____

NOTE

The *Navajo Language

The Navajo language, one of the Native American languages, also known as 'Diné Bizaad,' stands out as one of the world's most complex languages. ①Its *intricate structure and unique characteristics have made it a challenging language to master, and only a limited number of people *have a good command of it. Due to its complexity, the Navajo language was used as a *code during World War II, in which many Navajo
5　speakers were employed as 'Code Talkers' by the U.S. *military. They played a crucial role in the U.S. military by using their native language to create an *unbreakable code for sending crucial information securely on the battlefield.

Today, approximately 112 Native American languages remain in the United States, and many of them are spoken in communities called "*reservations." However, even in
10　these communities, the number of Native Americans who can speak their own languages is decreasing rapidly. More and more Native Americans use English, even within their homes, instead of their native language. ②This trend *holds true for the Navajo language, which has a larger number of speakers compared to many other Native American languages.

15　Manuelito Wheeler, the director of the *Navajo Nation Museum, recognized the urgent need to (　③　) the Navajo language and looked for some innovative solutions. Around 1996, Wheeler thought of the idea of *dubbing one of the *Star Wars* film series into Navajo. He was an *enthusiastic fan of the *Star Wars* series by George Lucas, and he thought that if Navajos could enjoy watching the great hit film with Navajo voices, it
20　would help *preserve the endangered language.

Wheeler organized a translation team and worked on translating the script of *Star Wars Episode IV: A New Hope* into Navajo. ［ア］ The translation itself took only less than 40 hours, but the negotiation with the movie's production companies did not proceed smoothly. ［イ］ It was not until the spring of 2012 that Disney and *Lucasfilm
25　agreed to support this ambitious project. ［ウ］ The Navajo version of *Star Wars Episode IV* made its debut during the 2012 Navajo Nation Fair, followed by screenings at various events across the country. ［エ］

In 2013, the Navajo-language version of *Star Wars Episode IV* was released on DVD. Wheeler hopes that this project's success will make the Navajo tribe members proud and encourage young Navajo individuals to become interested in their native language.

(403 words)

注：Navajo　ナバホ（部族名）　　　intricate　複雑な
　　have a good command of 〜　〜を使いこなす
　　code　暗号　　military　軍　　unbreakable　解読不可能な　　reservation　保留地
　　hold true for 〜　〜に当てはまる
　　Navajo Nation Museum　ナバホ部族博物館（＊この nation は「部族」の意）
　　dub　（映画のせりふなど）を吹き替える　enthusiastic　熱烈な
　　preserve　　〜を保存する
　　Lucasfilm　ルーカスフィルム（2012 年にウォルト・ディズニー・スタジオに買収された）

(1)　下線部①のような特性のために，ナバホ語は第二次世界大戦中にどのような目的のために使われたのか。30 字程度の日本語で説明しなさい。

　　＿＿＿＿＿＿＿＿＿＿＿＿＿＿＿＿＿＿＿＿＿＿＿＿＿＿＿＿＿＿＿＿＿ため。

(2)　下線部②の具体的内容となるように，（　　　　）を補い，日本文を完成させなさい。
　　アメリカ先住民族のコミュニティでは，（　　　　　　　　　　　　　　　　　　）人が
　　増えつつあるという傾向。

(3)　③に入る語として正しいものを 1 つ選び，記号で答えなさい。
　　ア　revitalize　　イ　suppress　　ウ　disrupt　　エ　ratify

　　　　　　　　　　　　　　　　　　　　　　　　　　　　　　（　　　）

(4)　以下の英文を補うのに適切な位置を，文中の[ア]〜[エ]から選び，記号で答えなさい。
　　Thousands of Navajo individuals had the opportunity to enjoy the film.

　　　　　　　　　　　　　　　　　　　　　　　　　　　　　　（　　　）

(5)　本文の内容と一致するものを 2 つ選び，記号で答えなさい。
　　ア　Many Navajo speakers were employed to break codes based on some complex languages during World War II.
　　イ　The Navajo language has the largest population of all Native American languages.
　　ウ　Manuelito Wheeler thought that dubbing *Star Wars Episode IV* into the Navajo native language might help preserve the language.
　　エ　Translating the script of Star Wars into Navajo took great amount of time because of the language's complexity.
　　オ　An increasing number of young Navajo individuals have learned their native language since the Navajo-version DVD of *Star Wars Episode IV* was released.

Useful Phrases & Idioms

My brother *is keen on playing* tennis.

I *got acquainted with* Mr. Smith at the party.
The doctor *dedicated himself to* cancer research.

The government worked *in cooperation with* the police.

Tom's father is *in charge of* the new project.

He *wreaked* his anger *on* the lazy office staff.
How did the car accident *come about*?
There was *an array of* famous singers at the festival.

The participants *varied in* age from fifteen to thirty.
4 *multiplied by* 6 is 24.

We *feasted on* delicious steak at the restaurant.
Rabbits *feed on* grass.

I didn't *eat a bite* of dinner last night.
She is *flushing* the sink *out* with warm water.

The couple *took* an orphan *in*.
Apart from his temper, he is a nice person.

The man was *convicted of* murder.
He was *sentenced to* 10 year's imprisonment.

There are no parks *in the vicinity of* my house.
That will *clear off* all her debts.

The United States *is composed of* 50 states.

We concluded the meeting *with a call* for peace.

The child *tore up* the newspaper.
Inflation has *been embedded in* the economy.

Students receive *hands-on* training with computers.
The kids are *munching on* sandwiches.

My sister always eats breakfast *on the run*.

☐ bring ~ into ...	They *brought* a law *into* force.
☐ spring up	Many restaurants have *sprung up* around my house.
☐ be well off	You'd *be better off* with me than with him.
☐ when it comes to ~	My father doesn't know anything *when it comes to* mechanics.
☐ to *one's* chagrin	*To his chagrin*, John failed to remember his promise.
☐ link ~ to ...	Improvements in health are *linked to* mental peace.
☐ induce ~ to *do*	She *induced* her father *to give* up smoking.
☐ inject ~ with ...	The doctor *injected* my arm *with* serum.
☐ catch up to ~	Tom ran as fast as he could to *catch up to* his brother.
☐ lag behind	This country *lags* far *behind* other countries in economics.
☐ kick-start	The government's attempt to *kick-start* the economy has succeeded.
☐ in effect	*In effect*, the two systems are almost the same.
☐ look into ~	You should *look into* the possibility.
☐ a shadow of doubt	There is no *shadow of doubt* that the woman is innocent.
☐ bond with ~	It is important for salesmen to *bond with* their clients.
☐ cast out	The woman was *cast out* from the club.
☐ run the risk of ~	I don't want to *run the risk of* losing my business.
☐ tear apart	The earthquake *tore* our newly-built house *apart*.
☐ pick up the pieces	It's my job to *pick up the pieces* when things go wrong.
☐ reckon with ~	Mr. Johnson is a man to be *reckoned with*.
☐ in an effort	I read those sentences over and over *in an effort* to memorize them.
☐ run its course	It took five days for the fever to *run its course*.
☐ accuse ~ of ...	He was *accused of* the crime.
☐ figure out	You have to *figure out* how to solve the problem for yourself.
☐ give out ~ to ...	We *gave out* leaflets *to* those who entered the hall.
☐ glance at ~	She *glanced* nervously *at* her watch.
☐ a fistful of ~	The boy is scooping up *a fistful of* sand.
☐ bear fruit	Her efforts *bore fruit*.
☐ on the rise	Prices are *on the rise* these days.

Ambition
English Communication III
Workbook

編集　開隆堂編集部
発行　開隆堂出版株式会社
　　　代表者　岩塚太郎
　　　〒113-8608　東京都文京区向丘1-13-1
　　　電話03-5684-6115（編集）
　　　https://www.kairyudo.co.jp/
印刷　株式会社大熊整美堂
販売　開隆館出版販売株式会社
　　　〒113-8608　東京都文京区向丘1-13-1
　　　電話03-5684-6118（販売）

■表紙デザイン
畑中 猛